PROGRESSIVE

Complete
Learn To Play
KEYBOARD
Manual

by
Peter Gelling and Gary Turner

Visit our Website
www.learntoplaymusic.com

The Progressive Series of Music Instruction Books, CDs and DVDs

Acknowledgments
Cover Photograph: Phil Martin
Photographs: Phil Martin

Special thanks to **Chris Martin**
for additional solos, as well as
his invaluable suggestions and proof reading.

For more information, contact:
LTP Publishing Pty Ltd.
Email: info@learntoplaymusic.com
or visit our web page at:
www.learntoplaymusic.com

I.S.B.N. 978-1-86469-237-2
Order Code: CP-69237

COPYRIGHT CONDITIONS
No part of this book can be reproduced in any form without written consent of the publisher.
© 2007 L.T.P. Publishing Pty Ltd

CONTENTS

CONTENTS CONTINUED

CONTENTS CONTINUED

CONTENTS CONTINUED

INTRODUCTION

Progressive COMPLETE LEARN TO PLAY KEYBOARDS Manual is the ultimate keyboard manual. It assumes you have no prior knowledge of music or playing keyboards and will take you **from beginner to professional level**. In the course of the book you will learn all the essential techniques for both piano and electronic keyboard playing, as well as how to read music and understand music theory up to an advanced level. You will also learn many well known pieces and songs and get a great introduction to many styles of music, including Rock, Blues, Jazz, Funk, Gospel, Folk and Classical.

The book is divided into sections, the first covering the basics of music reading and keyboard technique, concentrating on note memory and melody and accompaniment playing. The second section involves learning to move around on the keyboard and introduces a variety of new styles and techniques styles aimed at preparing you for group playing. The later sections deal with playing in all keys, transposing, chord substitution and Jazz playing.

All keyboard players should know all of the information contained in this book. By the end of the book, you will be an excellent keyboard player and will be ready for any musical situation you encounter. If you wish to pursue the study of Rock, Blues, Funk, Hip-Hop and related styles further, **Progressive COMPLETE LEARN TO PLAY ROCK AND BLUES KEYBOARDS Manual** is highly recommended.

APPROACH TO PRACTICE

It is important to have a correct approach to practice. You will benefit more from several short practices (e.g. 15-30 minutes per day) than one or two long sessions per week. This is especially so in the early stages, because of the basic nature of the material being studied. In a practice session you should divide your time evenly between the study of new material and the revision of past work. It is a common mistake for semi-advanced students to practice only the pieces they can already play well. Although this is more enjoyable, it is not a very satisfactory method of practice. You should also try to correct mistakes and experiment with new ideas. It is the author's belief that the guidance of an experienced teacher will be an invaluable aid in your progress.

USING THE COMPACT DISCS

This book comes with **two compact discs** which demonstrate almost all the examples in this book. The book shows you which notes, fingerings and techniques to use and the recording lets you hear how each example should sound. Practice the examples slowly along with a metronome at first, gradually increasing tempo. Once you are confident you can play the example evenly without stopping the beat, try playing along with the recording. You will hear a drum beat at the beginning of each example, to lead you into the example and to help you keep time. A small diagram of a compact disc with a number as shown below indicates a recorded example.

23.0 ← CD Track Number

HOW TO SIT AT THE KEYBOARD

Sit up straight and relaxed. If your seat can move up or down, adjust it to a comfortable height, see photo 1. The instrument shown here is an acoustic piano, but the sitting position is the same for all types of keyboard.

Photo 1

HAND SHAPE

Always curve your fingers. This helps keep your fingers at the same level, as shown in photo 2.

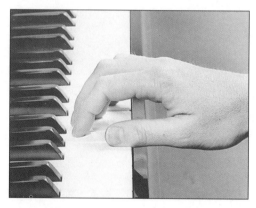

Photo 2

When you play the keys on the keyboard, use the tips of your fingers, and the side of your thumb. See photo 3.

Photo 3

MUSIC NOTES

There are only **seven** letters used for notes in music. They are:

A   B   C   D   E   F   G

These notes are known as the **musical alphabet**. They are the names of the **white** keys on the keyboard.

THE KEYBOARD

The black keys always appear in groups of two or three. The **C note** is a **white key**. It is always on the left hand side of a group of two black keys. Find all the **C** notes on your keyboard.

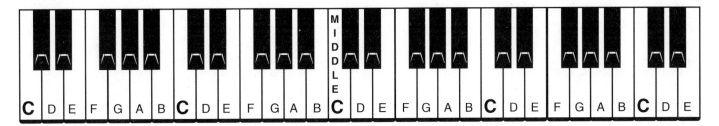

The first note you will learn to play is **Middle C**.

HOW TO FIND MIDDLE C

Middle C is the note in the middle of the keyboard. Play middle C with the thumb of your right hand, and then the thumb of your left hand.

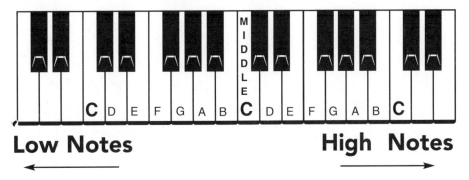

Low Notes   **High Notes**

Fingers

Each finger has its own number.

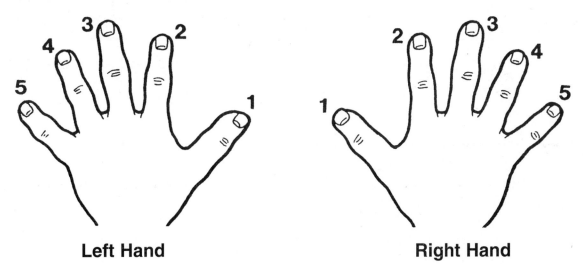

Left Hand   **Right Hand**

The **thumb** of each hand is counted as the **first** finger and has the number **1**.

HOW TO READ MUSIC

These five lines are called the **staff** or **stave**.
Music notes are written in the spaces and on the lines of the staff.

TREBLE CLEF

 This symbol is called a **treble clef**.

BASS CLEF

 This symbol is called a **bass clef**.

TREBLE STAFF

A staff with a treble clef written on it is called a **treble staff**.

BASS STAFF

A staff with a bass clef written on it is called a **bass staff**.

High notes are written on the **treble staff**, and are usually played with your **right hand**.
Low notes are written on the **bass staff**, and are usually played with your **left hand**.

THE GRAND STAFF

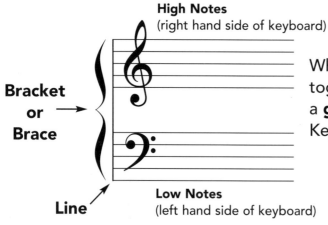

When the treble and bass staves are joined together by a line and a bracket, they are called a **grand staff**.
Keyboard music is written on the grand staff.

Music is divided into **bars** (sometimes called **measures**) by **bar lines**. In this example there are **two** bars of music.

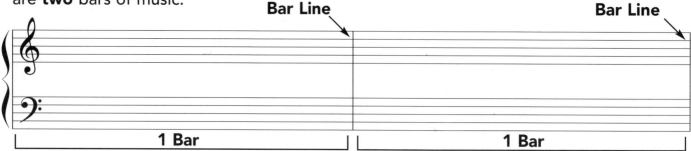

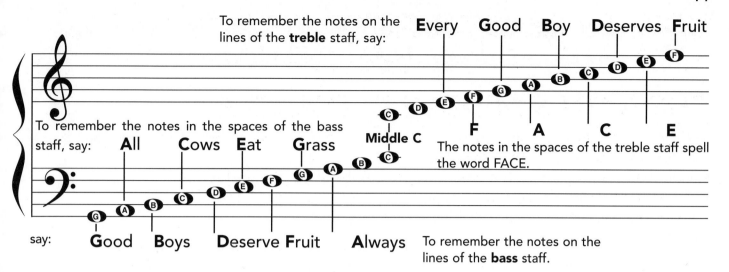

To remember the notes on the lines of the **treble** staff, say: Every Good Boy Deserves Fruit

To remember the notes in the spaces of the bass staff, say: All Cows Eat Grass

Middle C

The notes in the spaces of the treble staff spell the word FACE.

say: Good Boys Deserve Fruit Always

To remember the notes on the lines of the **bass** staff.

NOTE AND REST VALUES

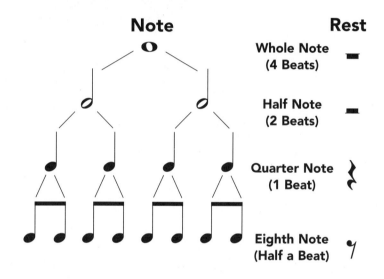

Note		Rest
	Whole Note (4 Beats)	
	Half Note (2 Beats)	
	Quarter Note (1 Beat)	
	Eighth Note (Half a Beat)	

THE QUARTER NOTE

stem

This is a musical note called a **quarter** note. A quarter note lasts for **one** beat.

note head

THE FOUR FOUR TIME SIGNATURE

The two pairs of numbers after the clefs are called the **time signature**.

This is called the **four four** time signature.

It tells you there are **four** beats in each bar. There are **four** quarter notes in a bar of ⁴₄ time.

LESSON ONE

THE NOTES MIDDLE C, D AND E

Middle C is written just **below** the treble staff on a short line called a **leger** line. See page 9 to locate middle C on the keyboard.
• Middle **C** is played with the **first** finger (thumb) of your right hand.
• The **D** note is played with the **second** finger of your right hand.
• The **E** note is played with the **third** finger of your right hand.

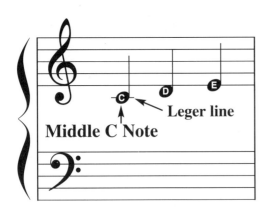

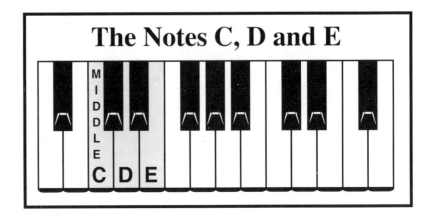

This is a **quarter** note. It lasts for **one** beat. There are **four** quarter notes in one bar of music in $\frac{4}{4}$ time.

Count: 1

 **1.0**

In the following example there are **four** bars of music, **two** bars of **middle C**, **one** bar of the **D** note and **one** bar of the **E** note. There are four quarter notes in each bar.

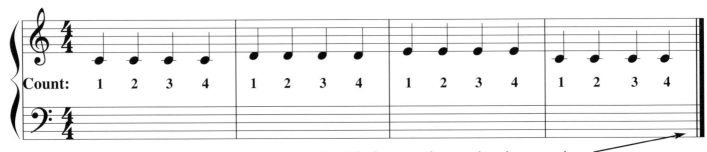

The **double bar** at the end indicates that the exercise has finished.

The Half Note

This is a **half** note. It lasts for **two** beats. There are **two** half notes in one bar of $\frac{4}{4}$ time.

Count: **1** 2

The Whole Note

This is a **whole** note. It lasts for **four** beats. There is **one** whole note in one bar of $\frac{4}{4}$ time.

Count: **1** 2 3 4

The **larger** bold numbers in the count indicate that a note is to be played. The **smaller** numbers indicate that a note is to be held until the next bold number (note).

1.1   In the Light of the Moon

This song contains quarter, half and whole notes. Make sure you use the correct fingers and follow the count carefully.

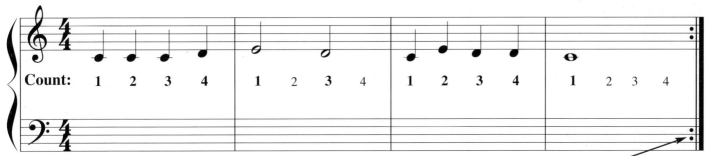

These two dots are a **repeat sign** and indicate that the piece is to be played again.

THE NOTES F AND G

The note **F** is played with the **fourth** finger of your right hand.
The note **G** is played with the **fifth** finger of your right hand.

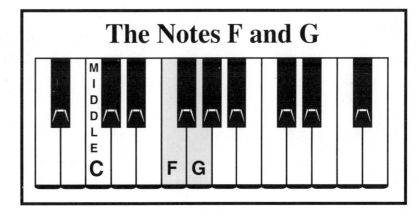

 1.2   Aura Lee

The song **Aura Lee** contains 8 bars of music in ⁴₄ time. Remember to count as you play, to help you keep time.

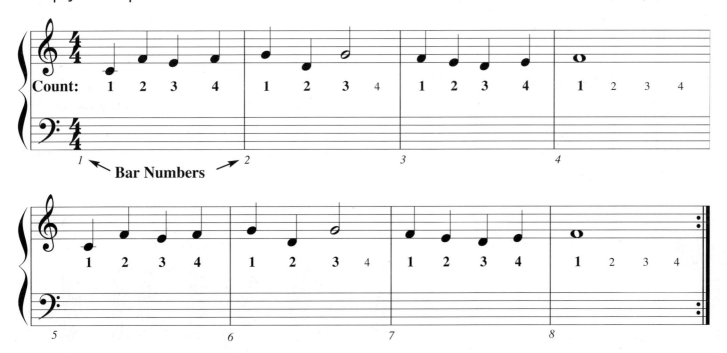

THINGS TO REMEMBER

1. Play the keys with the tips of your fingers.
2. Keep your fingers curved.

LESSON TWO

CHORDS

A **chord** is a group of notes which are played together. Chords are used to accompany the melody of a song. In the early stages, chords are usually played with the **left** hand and the melody is played with the right. The first chord you will learn is **C major**, usually just called the **C** chord.

THE C MAJOR CHORD

Chord Symbol

The **C** chord contains three notes - **C**, **E** and **G**. To play the **C** chord use the **first**, **third** and **fifth** fingers of your left hand, as shown in the **C** chord diagram.

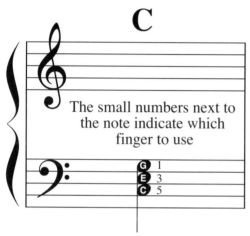

The small numbers next to the note indicate which finger to use

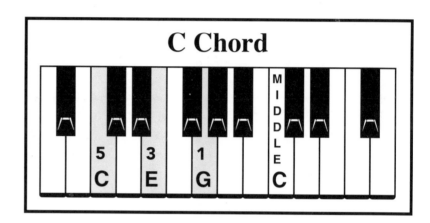

SEVENTH CHORDS

Another common type of chord is the **dominant seventh** chord, usually called a **seventh** chord. A seventh chord is indicated by the number **7** written after the chord name, eg: **G seventh** is written as **G7**.

Chord Symbol

THE G SEVENTH CHORD

The **G7** chord contains a new note - the **B** next to the C below Middle C. Play the B with the **fifth** finger of your left hand, and use your **first** and **second** fingers to play the G and F notes, as shown in the **G7** chord diagram.

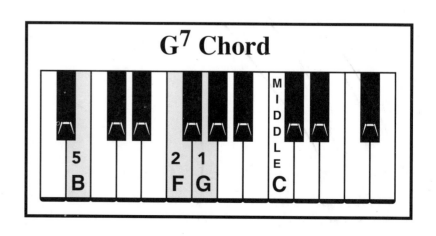

CHANGING CHORDS

Practice changing between the **C** and **G7** chords. As both these chords contain the same **G** note, changing between them is quite easy because the **thumb** stays in the same position. It is important to always use the correct fingering when playing notes and chords.

THE WHOLE REST

This symbol is a whole rest. It indicates **four** beats of silence in ₄⁴ time. **Small** counting numbers are placed under rests.

Count: 1 2 3 4
small numbers

 **2.0**

Chord symbols are placed above the staff. There are two chords in bar 3. Each chord receives **two** beats.

SONGS WITH CHORDS

Before playing songs with chords, practice each part separately. First practice the **melody** of the song by itself (right hand part), then practice the **chords** by themselves (left hand part). Once you have learnt both parts, play them together. Practice slowly and evenly, and count as you play. The part containing the chords is called the **accompaniment.**

 **2.1 Ode to Joy**

Ludwig van Beethoven

This song is the main theme to **Beethoven's 9th Symphony**. It contains all the notes and chords you have learnt so far and has two chords in bar 8.

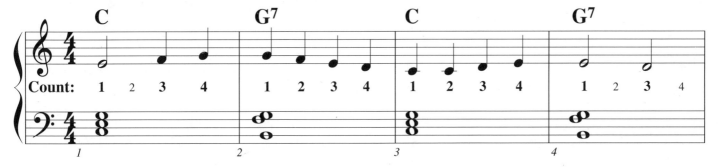

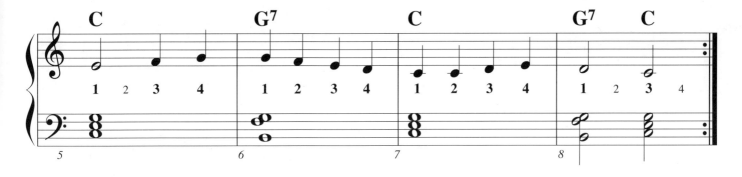

LESSON THREE

THE QUARTER REST

 This symbol is a quarter rest. It indicates **one beat of silence**. Do not play any note. Remember that small counting numbers are placed under rests.

Count: 1

 2.2 **Good Evening Friends**

Count: 1
One beat of silence

Chord Symbol

The F Chord

The next chord you will learn to play is the **F** chord. To play the **F** chord, use the **first**, **second** and **fifth** fingers of your left hand, as shown in the F chord diagram. The **F** chord introduces the note **A** below middle C.

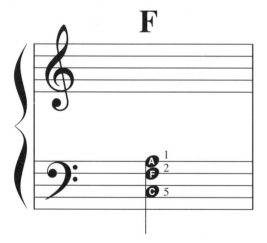

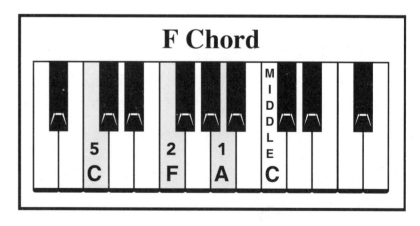

When changing between the **C** and **F** chords keep your **fifth** finger in position as this note is common to both chords. When changing between the **F** and **G7** chords keep your **second** finger in position as this note is common to both chords. Practice changing between **C**, **F** and **G7**.

THE HALF REST

This is a **half** rest. It indicates **2 beats** of silence.

Count: 1 2

THE LEAD-IN

Sometimes a song does not begin on the first beat of a bar. Any notes which come before the first full bar are called **lead-in notes** (or **pick-up notes**). When lead-in notes are used, the last bar is also incomplete. The notes in the lead-in and the last bar add up to one full bar.

3. When the Saints go Marchin' in

When the Saints Go Marchin' In is a Jazz standard made popular by brass bands in New Orleans.The song uses a lead-in and also contains both quarter and half rests. The **counting numbers** refer to the **melody** (right hand part).
Instead of writing a chord symbol above each bar of music it is common to only write a chord symbol when the chord changes, e.g. the first 6 bars of this song use a **C** chord.

LESSON FOUR

THE THREE FOUR TIME SIGNATURE

This time signature is called the **three four** time signature. It indicates that there are **three** beats in each bar. Three four time is also known as waltz time. There are **three** quarter notes in one bar of ¾ time.

THE DOTTED HALF NOTE

A dot written after a note extends its value by half.
A dot after a half note means that you hold it for **three** beats.
One dotted half note makes one bar of music in ¾ time.

Count: 1 2 3

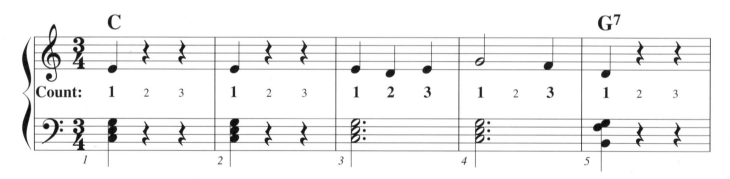

4. Austrian Waltz

This song has dotted half notes in the left hand part. Once again, the counting numbers refer to the melody (right hand part). The left hand part is the **accompaniment** to the melody.

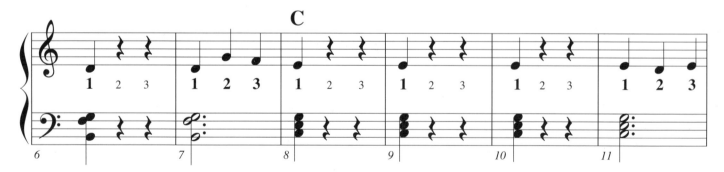

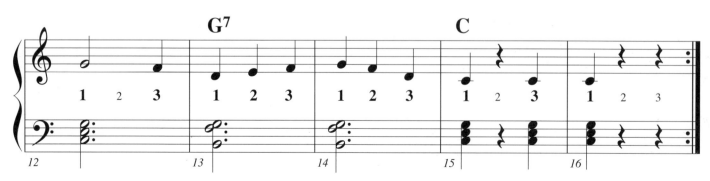

THE TIE

A **tie** is a curved line that connects two notes with the **same** position on the staff. A tie tells you to play the **first** note only, and to hold it for the length of both notes.

 **5.0**

Play the **C** note and chord and hold them for **six** beats.

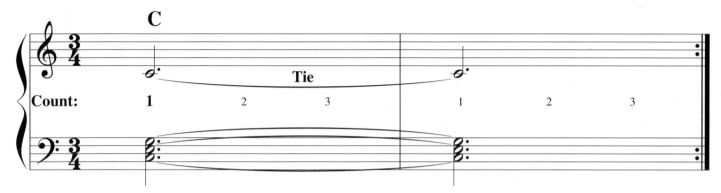

 **5.1 Marianne**

This Caribbean folk song contains several ties which go across the bar line. Using ties is the only way of indicating that a note should be held across a bar line. Take care with the timing of the left hand part in this song.

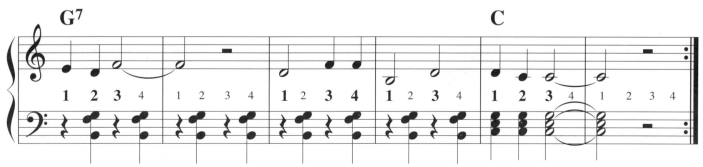

LESSON FIVE

THE NOTES A, B AND C

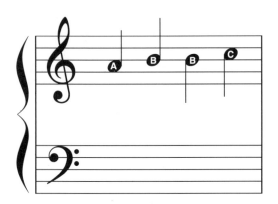

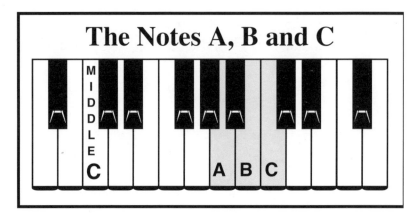

Notes written **above** the middle line of a staff usually have their stems going **down.** Notes written **below** the middle line of the staff usually have their stems going **up.** The stem for the **B** note can go **up or down.**

THE C MAJOR SCALE

A **major scale** is a group of eight notes that gives the familiar sound:

Do Re Mi Fa So La Ti Do

You now know enough notes to play the **C major scale**. To play the scale smoothly you will need to play the **F** note with your **thumb.** Do this by moving your thumb **underneath** your second and third fingers on the way **up** the scale. On the way **down** the scale, move your second and third fingers **over** your thumb. This is called the **crossover.**

The small numbers placed above, below or beside notes on the staves tell you which finger to play each note with. Be sure to use the correct finger.

CD 1 6.0

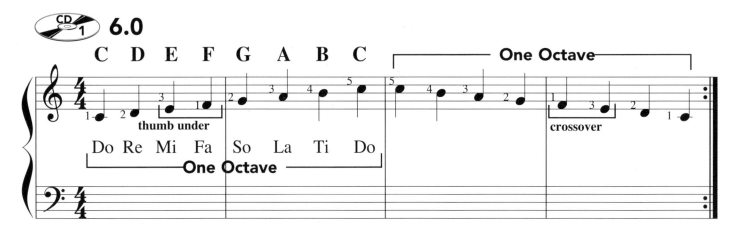

THE OCTAVE

An **octave** is the range of eight notes of a major scale. The **first** note and the **last** note of a major scale always have the **same** name. In the C major scale, the distance from Middle C to the C note above it (or below it) is one octave (eight notes). All the songs you have studied so far, and the next song use notes from the C major scale. Pay close attention to any fingering numbers near the notes. It is important to use the indicated fingering, as this will make the songs easier to play. Use this same fingering every time you play the songs.

6.1   La Spagnola

La Spagnola uses notes from the **C major scale** and uses the **thumb under** between bars **20** and **21.**

THE EIGHTH NOTE

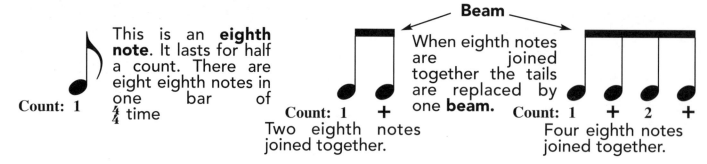

This is an **eighth note**. It lasts for half a count. There are eight eighth notes in one bar of $\frac{4}{4}$ time

Count: 1

Beam

When eighth notes are joined together the tails are replaced by one **beam**.

Count: 1 +
Two eighth notes joined together.

Count: 1 + 2 +
Four eighth notes joined together.

7.0   How to Count Eighth Notes

Written:	1	+	2	+	3	+	4	+
Count:	1	and	2	and	3	and	4	and

STACCATO

A **dot** placed above or below a note tells you to play it **staccato**. Staccato means to play a note short and separate from the other notes. To play a note short, lift your finger off the keys as quickly as possible.

7.1   Shave and a Haircut

There are two eighth notes on the second beat of the first bar of this example. Play the notes and chords in the second bar staccato.

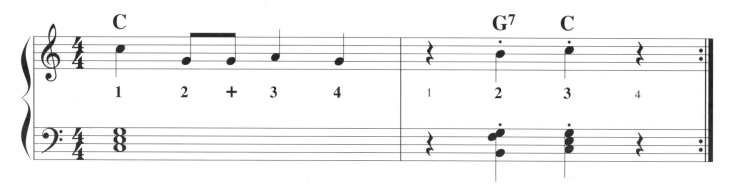

KEY OF C MAJOR

When a song consists of notes from a particular scale, it is said to be written in the **key** which has the **same** name as that scale. For example, if a song contains notes from the **C major scale**, it is said to be in the **key of C major**. Nearly all the songs you have studied so far have been in the key of C major.

8. Lavender's Blue

This well known English folk song is in the key of **C major**. It uses a crossover in bar **14**.

LESSON SIX

THE DOTTED QUARTER NOTE

A dot written after a quarter note indicates that you should hold the note for **one and a half beats**. A dotted quarter note is often followed by an eighth note.

Count 1   2   +

 9.0

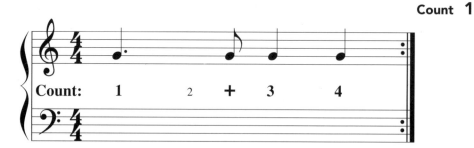

 **9.1   Lullaby**

Johannes Brahms

Brahms' Lullaby is one of the most well known melodies of all time. It is written here in the key of **C major** and uses dotted quarter notes in bars 1, 3, 9 and 13.

FIRST AND SECOND ENDINGS

The next song contains **first and second endings**. The **first** time you play through the song, play the **first** ending, (1.⌐ ⌐), then go back to the beginning. The **second** time you play through the song, play the **second** ending (2.⌐ ⌐) instead of the first.

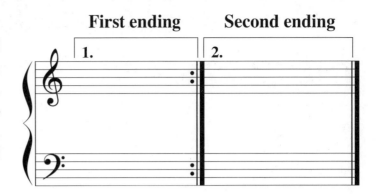

 9.2 Jingle Bells

Jingle Bells is one of the most popular christmas songs. It contains first and second endings. The first time through, play from the beginning to the end of bar **8**. Then play again from the beginning, but this time **do not** play bars 7 and 8 (the first ending) but play bars **9** and **10** (the second ending).

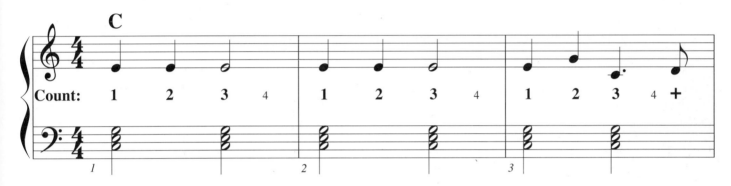

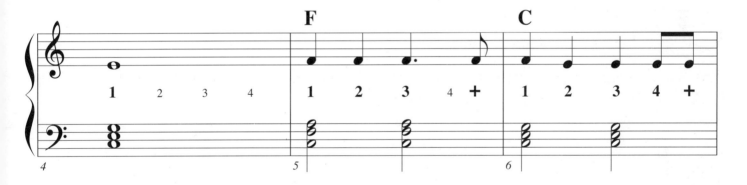

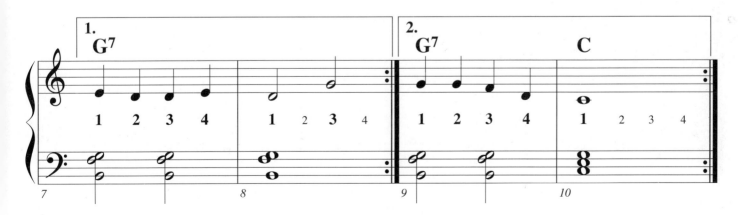

LESSON SEVEN

THE BASS STAFF

Looking at the keyboard you can see that the same notes are repeated many times. So far you have learnt the notes **C D E F** and **G** on the treble staff, all played with the right hand. Notes played by the **left** hand are usually notated on the **bass staff**. Shown below are the notes C D E F and G on the bass staff. These notes sound exactly one **octave** lower than the same five notes in the treble staff.

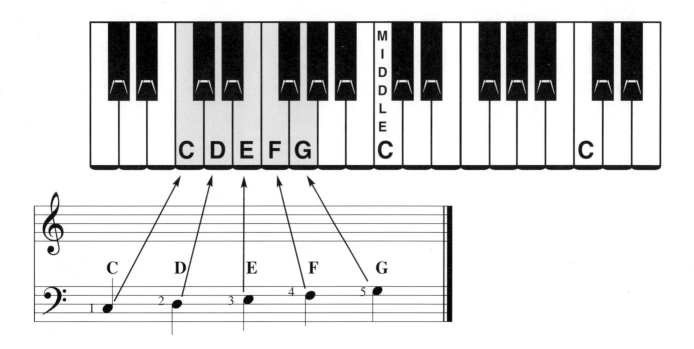

 **10.0   Aura Lee**

Here is the first part of the song Aura Lee written in the bass staff and then the treble staff. Sing the names of the notes out loud as you play them.

Now play the following example which uses both hands together. Listen carefully and try to play the notes with both hands at the same time rather than being slightly separate or split.

CD 1 10.1

PLAYING CHORDS WITH THE RIGHT HAND

It is also important to be able to play single notes with the left hand while playing **chords** with the **right hand**. The **G7** chord is played with the first, fourth and fifth fingers.

CD 1 10.2

PLAYING SCALES WITH BOTH HANDS

The following example demonstrates the C major scale played with the left hand and then both hands together. The left hand fingering is the reverse of that of the right hand. The crossover occurs between **G** and **A**. When playing the scale with both hands together, the crossovers occur at different times with each hand, so take care not to lose your timing at these points. Play very slowly at first and only increase the speed once you can play the whole example smoothly and evenly.

11.0

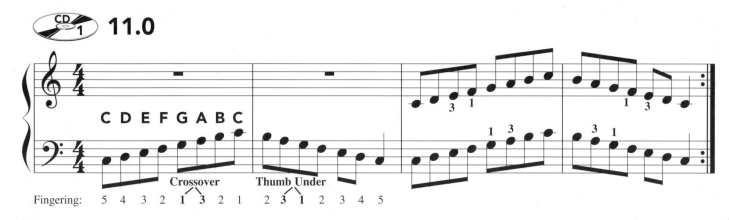

11.1   Lavender's Blue (Melody in Bass)

Here is a new version of the song you learned in lesson 5. This time the melody is played with the left hand. Practice each hand separately if you need to.

LESSON EIGHT

MINOR CHORDS

There are three main types of chords: **major**, **seventh** and **minor** chords. You have already learnt one major chord and one seventh chord. The first **minor** chord you will learn is the **D minor** chord. Minor chords are indicated by a small "m" written after the chord name, e.g. **Dm.**

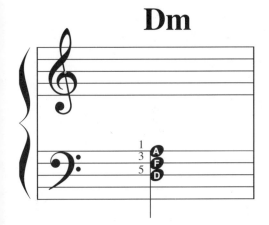

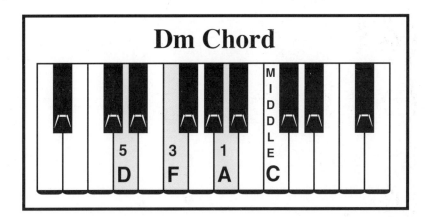

To play the **D minor** chord, use the **first**, **third** and **fifth** fingers of your left hand. Once you are confident you know the chord, play it one octave higher with the right hand. As with the major chords, the fingering will be reversed for the right hand.

12.0

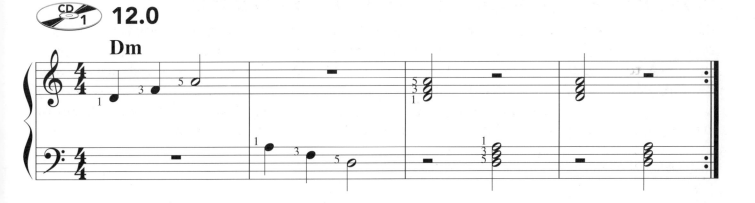

12.1

Next, practice changing between the chords **Dm** and **C**. Remember that the fingering is the same for both chords but the whole hand moves.

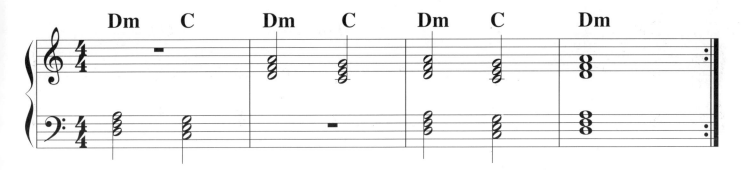

FIVE FINGER POSITIONS

In the following example the right hand plays the melody while the left hand provides the accompaniment with the chords Dm and C. Notice the position of the right hand, with the thumb on the note D and the other fingers covering the notes E, F, G and A. This is often referred to as the D five finger position, or **D position** for short. Many of the previous examples have covered the notes C, D, E, F and G. This is known as the **C position**.

13.0

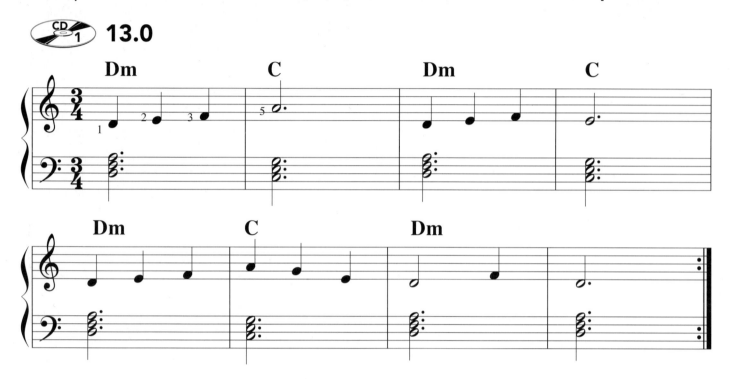

KEYBOARD VOICES AND "TIMBRE"

In the next piece both hands shift between the D position and the C position. On the recording, this example is played with an **organ** voice. This means the sound has a different tone quality (called "**timbre**") to that of a piano voice. Each instrument and human voice has its own particular timbre. Certain parts can sound great when played by one instrument, but terrible when the wrong one is used. Experiment with different instrumental voices on your keyboard when playing all the examples in the book.

13.1

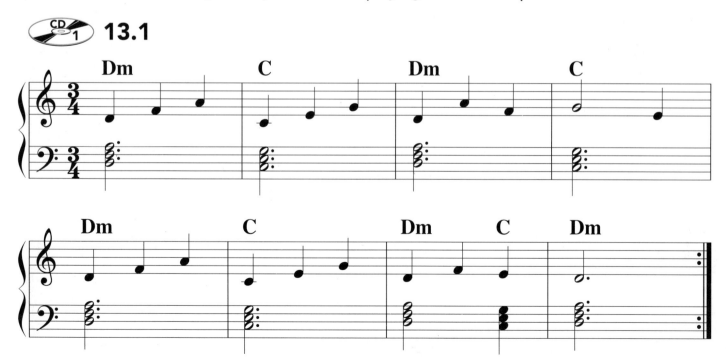

THE A MINOR CHORD

Am

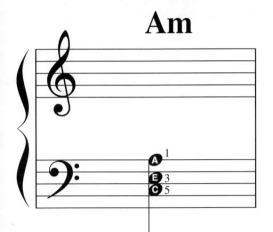

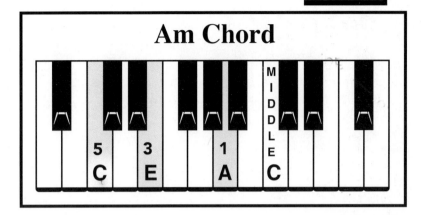

THE E MINOR CHORD

Em

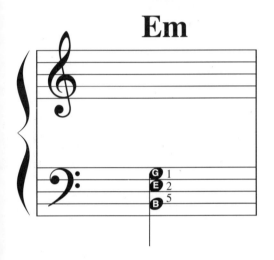

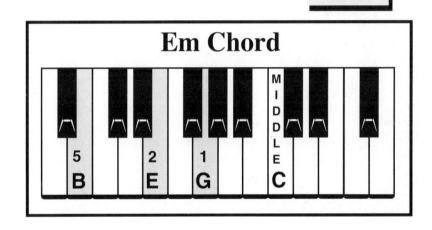

CD 1 **13.2**

This example uses the chords **Am**, **Dm** and **Em**. The final bar contains two new low **A** notes, one played by each hand.

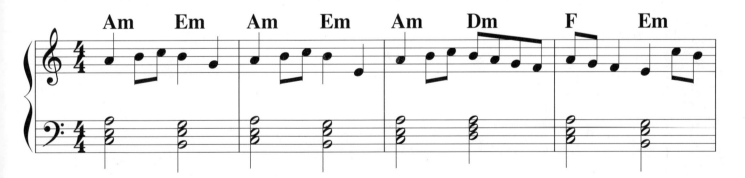

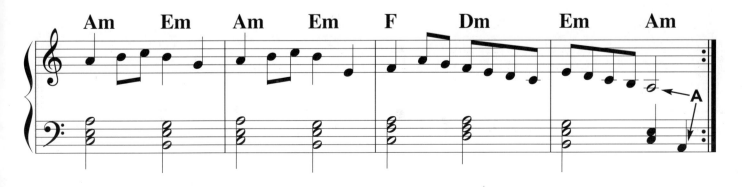

LESSON NINE

ARPEGGIOS

An arpeggio is a chord played one note at a time. Arpeggios can be played by either hand and any chord can be played as an arpeggio. The following example demonstrates the chords **Dm** and **C** played as arpeggios.

 **14.0**

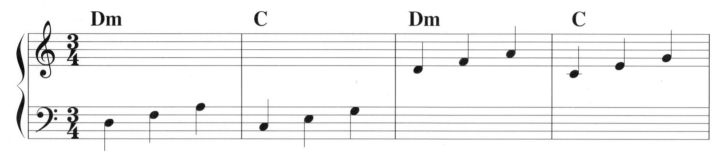

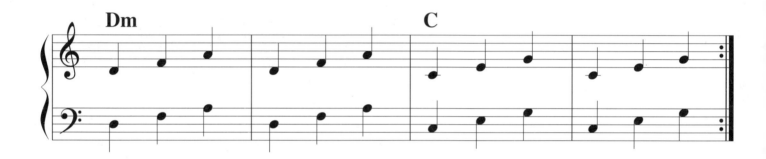

 **14.1**

Arpeggios are often used by the left hand to accompany a melody played by the right hand.

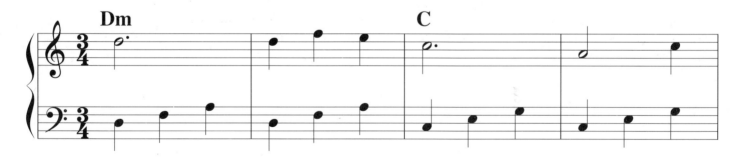

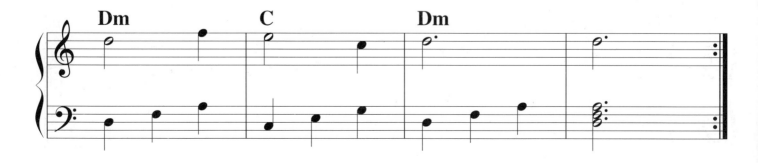

 **15. Scarborough Fair**

Scarborough Fair is a folk music standard. The accompaniment in this arrangement consists of arpeggios of the chords **Dm**, **C** and **F** played by the left hand. Take it slowly at first and practice each hand separately if you need to.

16.   Chopsticks

Chopsticks is one of the most well known beginner's pieces for piano. If your hand is not big enough to stretch the octave in bar 7 you can play the whole right hand part of the song using two hands. The left hand part consists of arpeggios of the chords **C** and **G7**. Practice each hand separately at first if you have trouble co-ordinating the two parts. This song is in the key of **C major** as indicated by the key signature (i.e. no sharps or flats).

BROKEN CHORDS

Another common style of accompaniment is the use of Broken chords. This style is similar to arpeggio playing except that the lowest note of the chord is the only one played by itself. The following example demonstrates broken chords in 4/4 time.

17.1   Oh Susanna

This traditional American folk song is played with a broken chord accompaniment. Once you can play it, try applying broken chord accompaniments to other songs you know.

LESSON TEN

SHARP SIGNS

 This is a **sharp** sign.
When a sharp sign is placed before a note on the staff, it indicates that you play the key immediately to its **right.** This key may be either **black** or **white.**

THE D7 CHORD

The **D7** chord contains an **F sharp** note which is the black key immediately to the **right** of the F note (white key) below middle C. This **F♯** note is written on the **fourth** line of the bass staff. To play the **D7** chord, use the **first, third** and **fourth** fingers of your left hand as shown in the **D7** chord diagram.

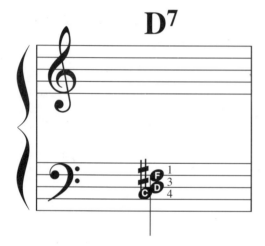

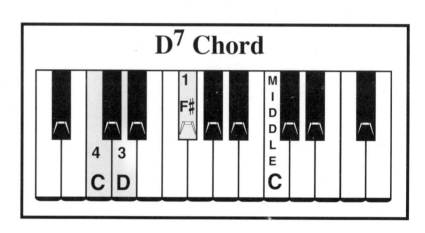

18.0

In this example, the **D7** chord is played by the left hand until the final bar, where it is played by the right hand. Practice changing between **D7** and **C** with both hands.

THE G CHORD

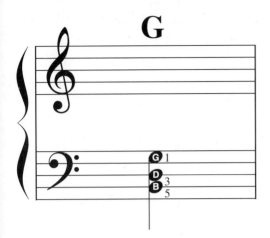

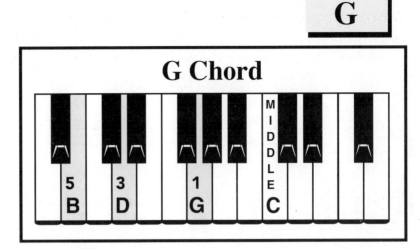

To play the **G** chord, use the **first**, **third** and **fifth** fingers of your left hand, as shown in the **G** chord diagram.

18.1   Hush Little Baby

The accompaniment to this popular children's song features **G** and **D7** played as broken chords.

19. Morning Has Broken

Morning Has Broken uses all the chords you have learnt so far and is played with an arpeggio style accompaniment. If you have trouble co-ordinating both hands, practice each hand separately until you are confident playing each part and then combine them.

THE NOTE F♯ (above Middle C)

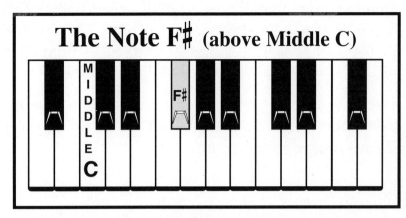

This **F♯** note is written in the **first space** of the treble staff.

This **F♯** note is the **black** key immediately to the **right** of the F note as shown in the diagram.

20.0 **The William Tell Overture** G. Rossini

Most of the notes and chords in this song are played **staccato** as indicated by the dot placed under or over the note.

HIGHER C POSITION

Continuing on with the concept of naming five finger hand positions from the lowest note, it is possible to quickly learn new notes. You have already learnt all the natural notes used in music: **A B C D E F** and **G**. As you know, each of these notes is repeated many times up and down the keyboard in different octaves.

Find the note **C** one octave above middle C with the first finger (thumb) of your right hand. Your remaining fingers will be covering the notes D, E, F and G. These notes are shown below on the treble staff.

20.1   Ode to Joy (Higher)

Here is the full melody of Ode to Joy using the notes from the new higher C position. Notice the alternating bass notes in the left hand part. This simple but effective form of accompaniment is used in many styles of music.

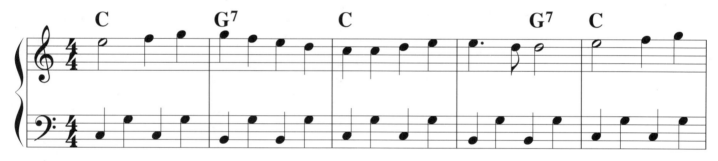

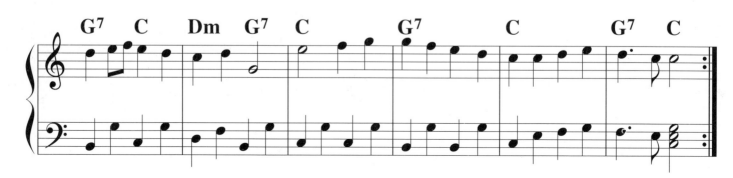

21. Springtime Melody

This piece summarises most of the things covered in the book up to this point. You now know eight chords and all of the different notes available on the white keys. Use what you have learnt to experiment and start creating some of your own music.

LEGATO

The next song contains curved lines called **slurs.** A slur indicates that the notes written above or below it, should be played **legato.** Legato means to play the notes smoothly, so that they sound connected to each other. Legato is the opposite of staccato. To play notes legato, keep your finger on the key until you have started to play the next key. This song also introduces a new high **F#** note one octave above the F# note you already know.

 22.0 Sliding Down

 22.1 Stepping and Sliding

This one contains the same notes as the previous example, but this time some of the notes are played staccato. When one hand is playing staccato it is easy to let the other hand follow. However, none of the chords here are played staccato. Practice each part separately if necessary.

LESSON ELEVEN

THE G MAJOR SCALE

In Lesson 5 the C Major scale was introduced. The **G major scale** starts and ends on the note **G**, and contains an **F♯** note instead of an F note. Play the following G major scale and notice that it still has the familiar sound **Do Re Mi Fa So La Ti Do**.

KEY SIGNATURES

The key of C major was discussed in lesson 5. Songs that use notes from the **C major scale** are said to be in the **key of C major**. Similarly, songs that use notes from the **G major scale** are said to be in the **key of G major**. Songs in the key of G will usually contain **F♯** notes.

Instead of writing a sharp sign before every F note on the staff, it is easier to write just **one** sharp sign after each clef. This means that **all** the F notes on the staff are played as **F♯**, even though there is no sharp sign written before them. This is called a **key signature**.

This is the key signature for the key of **G major**. It has **one** sharp sign after each clef

The C major scale contains no sharps or flats, therefore the key signature for the key of **C major** contains **no** sharps or flats.

23. The Galway Piper

This song is a traditional Irish dance tune, written here in the key of **G major**. Notice the key signature reminding you to play all F notes as **F♯**. The left hand accompaniment contains broken chords played **staccato.** Take care when changing from **G** to **D7** and practice the left hand by itself if you need to.

PRACTICING SCALES

As Mentioned previously, it is essential to be able to play both single notes and chords equally well with both hands. A good way of developing strength and independence in all the fingers is to practice scales with each hand and with both hands together. Shown below are various ways of playing the G major scale. First, here is the scale in the bass staff - to be played by the left hand. The first note is a new low G note. Notice the fingering written under the music - a crossover is necessary when moving between **D** and **E**.

24.0   Left Hand

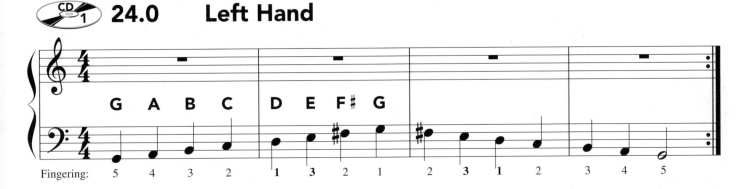

24.1   Both Hands

Next, play the scale with both hands together. Play slowly and listen carefully. Don't rush! The most important thing is to play each note with both hands at exactly the same time, and to be sure all notes are even in length and volume. This time the right hand part begins with a new low G note. The crossovers occur at different times with each hand, so take care not to lose your timing at these points.

Once you can play a scale smoothly and evenly with both hands together, the next step is to play it over more than one octave. The following example shows the G major scale played in eighth notes over two octaves. The first note of the second octave is played with the thumb (1). This necessitates thumb under and crossover techniques. Take them slowly at first and only increase the speed once it is totally comfortable.

24.2   Both Hands Over Two Octaves

THE COMMON TIME SIGNATURE

 This symbol is called **common time**. It means exactly the same as $\frac{4}{4}$.

 25. Changing Lanes

This example in common time will put your scale practice to good use. The melody is played first by the left hand and then the right. The hands reverse roles every four bars.

LESSON TWELVE

FLAT SIGNS

♭ This is a **flat** sign.

When a **flat sign** is placed before a note on the staff, it means that you play the key immediately to its **left**. This key may be either black or white. The note **B flat** (written as B♭) is shown on the staff below in both treble and bass.

THE NOTE B♭
(Treble and Bass)

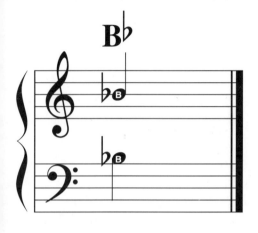

These B♭ notes are written on the **third** line of the **treble staff** and the **second** line of the **bass staff**.

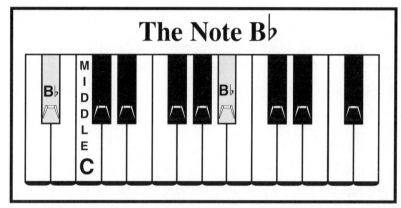

The B♭ note is the **black** key immediately to the left of the B note, as shown in the diagram.

26.0 Ghost of the Moor

This piece uses both the B♭ notes shown above. Playing single note lines with both hands is often more difficult than a melody accompanied by chords. Practice each hand separately if you need to.

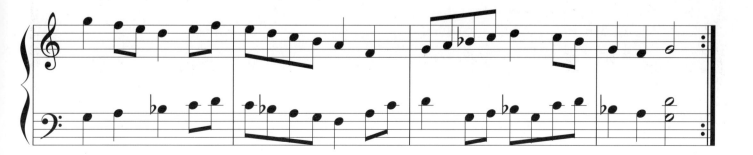

THE C7 CHORD

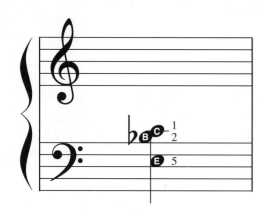

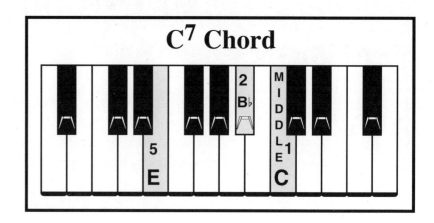

26.1

Practice changing between the chords **F** and **C7** with both hands as shown below.

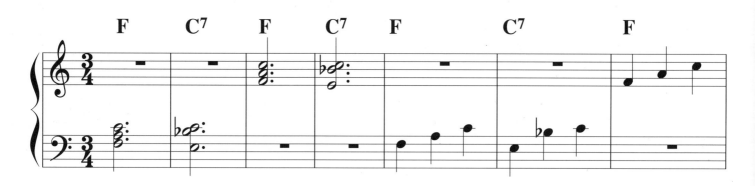

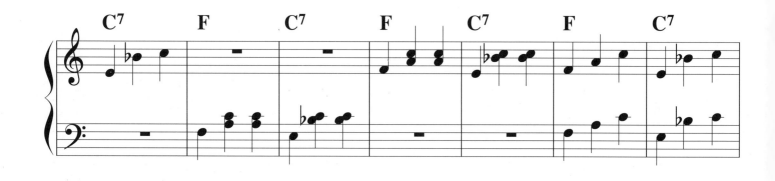

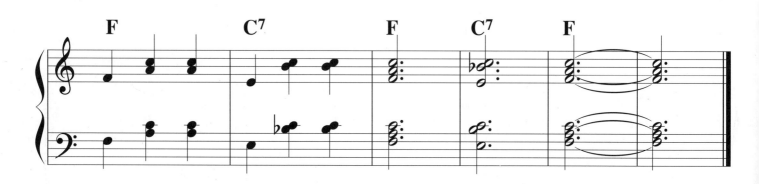

KEY SIGNATURE OF F MAJOR

Instead of writing the flat sign before every B note on the staff, **one flat sign can be written after each clef.** This means that **all** B notes on the staff are played as **B♭**, even though there is no flat sign written before them. This is the key signature for the **key of F major**. There is **one** flat sign after each clef.

 **27. Austrian Waltz**

Here is a new version of the song you learnt in lesson 4, this time in the key of **F major**. Notice the use of **F** and **C7** played as broken chords in the left hand part.

The B♭ Chord

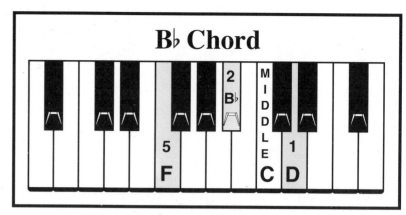

To play the **B♭** chord, use the first, second and fifth fingers of your left hand as shown in the **B♭** chord diagram. Practice changing between **F** and **B♭** and also **B♭** and **C7**.

28. Shortnin' Bread

Notice the quick changes between **F** and **B♭** in this song. This style of accompaniment is common in Blues and Boogie piano playing. These styles will be dealt with later in the book.

THE F MAJOR SCALE

The **F major scale** starts and ends on the note **F**, and it contains a **B♭** note instead of a B note. Play the F major scale below and listen for the **Do Re Mi Fa So La Ti Do** sound. Songs that use notes from the F major scale are in the **key of F major** and hence contain the note **B♭**. When playing the F major scale, take care with the fingering as the crossover point is different to that of the C and G major scales.

29.0

29.1

Here is the F major scale played over two octaves with both hands. It begins with two new **F** notes. To become familiar with the notes of the scale, name the notes out loud as you play. Memorize the fingering, and take care with the crossover points in both hands, and practice each hand individually as well as both together. As always, clarity and evenness are more important than speed.

 **30.** **The Mountain Stream**

This song is in the key of **F major** and contains a variation on the broken chord style of accompaniment. As with previous examples, practice each hand separately if you need to.

SECTION 2
Using the Whole Keyboard

LESSON THIRTEEN

USING THE WHOLE KEYBOARD

So far you have learnt notes from a low F to a high G covering a range of just over 3 octaves. By learning the new notes shown on the staff and keyboard below you will be able to play over a range of **4 octaves**, which covers most music.

31.0

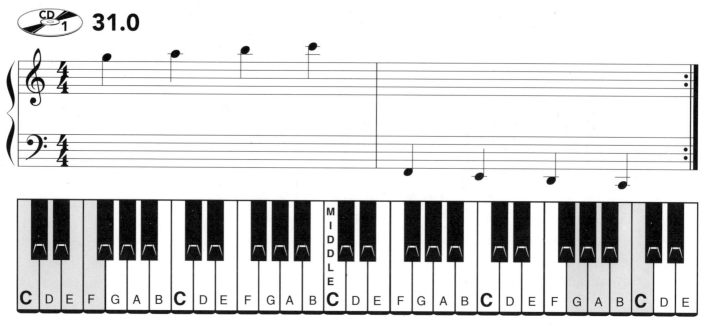

31.1

Now try playing a C major scale over four octaves. The low C shown here is the lowest note on some keyboards, but not on a piano or full length keyboard .

31.2   The 8va Symbol

The following phrase has the symbol **8va** above the music. This means it is played an octave higher than written. This symbol is often used for very high notes, as it makes them easier to read. When the notation returns to its normal pitch, the word **loco** is written above the music.

CHORD INVERSIONS

So far you have learnt the C, F and G major chords. Because the lowest note in each of these three chords is the root note, the shape given is called the **root position**.

All major chords contain three different notes. These notes can be duplicated and/or played in a different shape. When the third (3) is the lowest note of the chord shape, the chord is said to be the **first inversion**. The diagram below illustrates the first inversion of the **C major** chord, which contains the notes **E** (3), **G** (5), and **C** (1) in that order.

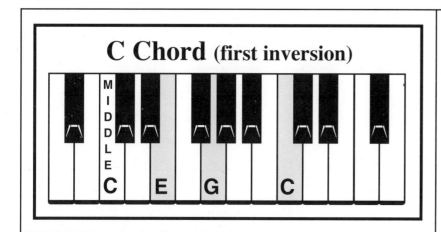
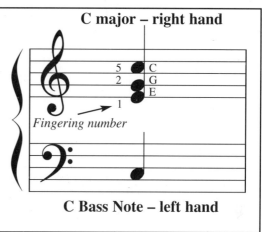

Do not confuse the fingering numbers on the chord diagrams with the interval numbers of the chord.

When the fifth (5) is the lowest note of the chord shape, the chord is said to be the **second inversion**. The diagram below illustrates the second inversion of the C major chord, which contains the notes **G** (5), **C** (1), and **E** (3) in that order.

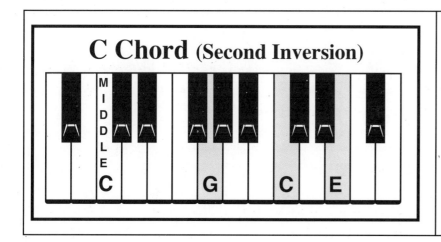
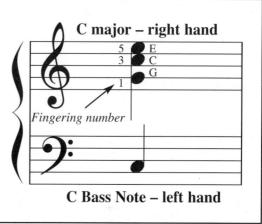

C MAJOR CHORD INVERSIONS

The example below uses root position, first inversion, second inversion, and an octave of the root position of the C chord in the right hand part. Use the correct right fingering as shown on the notation accompanying the diagrams.

32.0

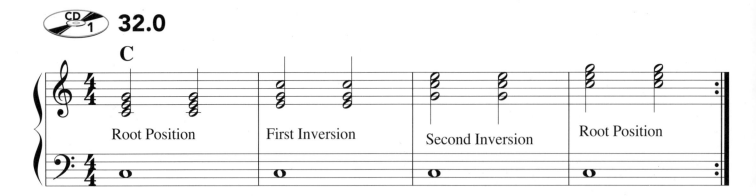

G MAJOR CHORD INVERSIONS

These three diagrams illustrate the root position (1 3 5), first inversion (3 5 1), and second inversion (5 1 3) of the G chord.

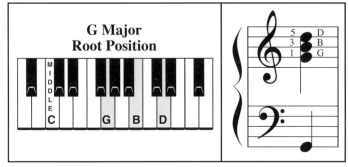

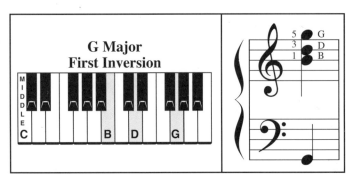

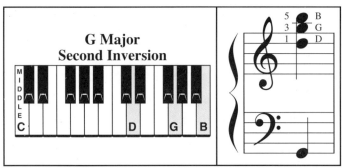

The following example uses the root position, first inversion, second inversion, and an octave of the root position of the G chord. Once again, remember to use the correct fingering as shown in the notation alongside the diagrams.

32.1

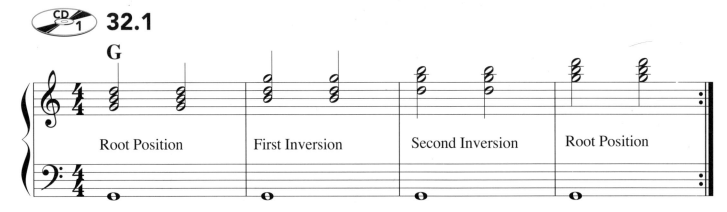

F MAJOR CHORD INVERSIONS

These three diagrams illustrate the root position (1 3 5), first inversion (3 5 1), and second inversion (5 1 3) of the F chord.

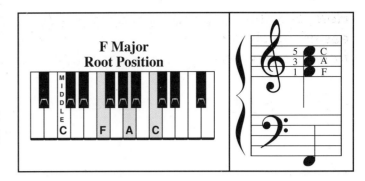

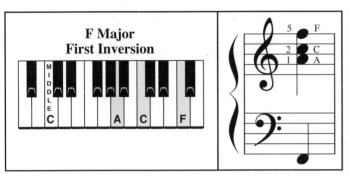

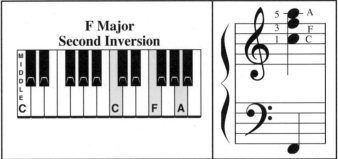

32.2

This example shows the root position, first inversion, second inversion, and an octave of the root position of the **F** chord.

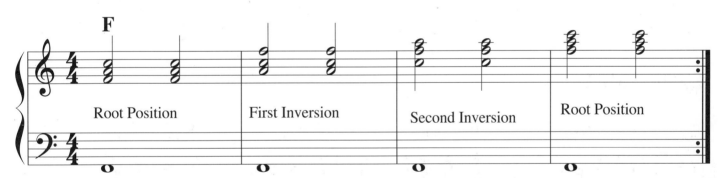

32.3

One of the reasons inversions are so useful is that they enable you to find chord shapes which are close together on the keyboard. Here the **C** chord appears in **root position**, the **F** chord is in **second inversion** and the **G** chord is in **first inversion.** The left hand plays the root note of each chord.

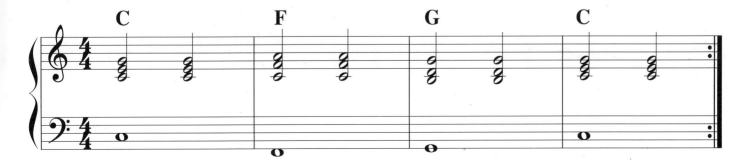

Here are some examples showing typical uses of these inversions. Notice how much easier the chord changes are. By using inversions which are close together, it leaves you free to concentrate on other important things such as rhythm.

33.0

33.1

33.2

TEMPO MARKINGS

The term **tempo** refers to the **speed** at which music is played. As with dynamic markings, tempo markings come from Italian words. Some of them are listed below, along with their English translations. It is important to be able to recognize these markings and to be able to play comfortably at each tempo.

Adagio (slowly)   **Andante** (an easy walking pace)   **Moderato** (a moderate speed)

Allegro (fast)   **Presto** (very fast)

 34.   Waltzing Inversions

Moderato

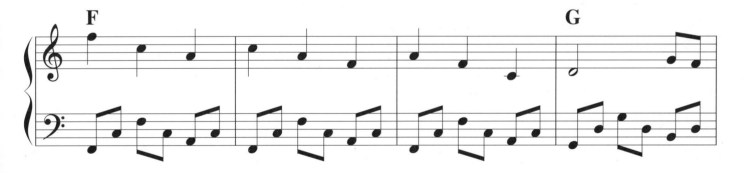

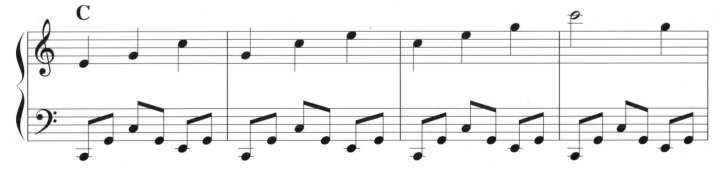

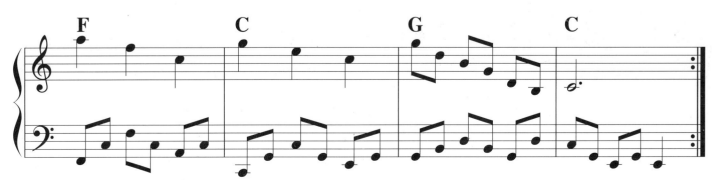

CLASSICAL STUDIES

Regardless of the style of music you intend to play as your first preference, you can learn a lot by studying Classical music. The term "Classical" is very general and covers many periods and styles of music spanning hundreds of years. There are many great pieces and studies by a variety of composers which will help you develop a solid technique and a good understanding of how scales and chords work together to make music. A list of suggested studies is given on page 113. The following example is a study by **Carl Czerny**, who was one of Beethoven's teachers. Notice that the chords played by the left hand are written on a treble staff. Although the tempo marking is **Allegro**, take it slowly until you can play it comfortably.

 **35.** **Study by Czerny**

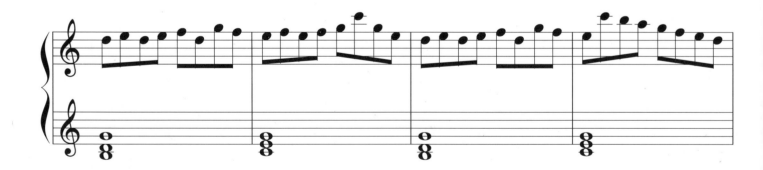

LESSON FOURTEEN

THE EIGHTH REST

This symbol is an **eighth rest.** It indicates **half a beat** of silence.

Here is an example which makes use of eighth rests on the first and third beats in the right hand part. Be sure to keep your timing steady with the left hand and count as you play.

36.0

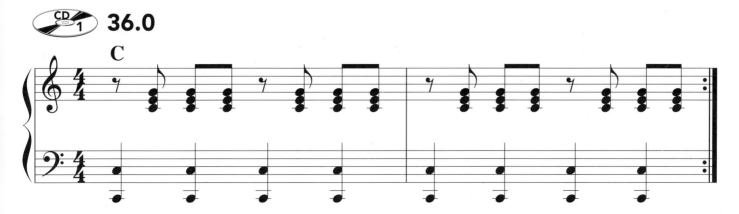

SYNCOPATION

In the following example all the eighth notes are played off the beat. Playing off the beat creates an effect known as **syncopation**, which means displacing the normal flow of accents (usually from on the beat to off the beat). Syncopated rhythms can be difficult at first but are common in many styles of music, so stick with it. Count and tap your foot to keep time as you play.

36.1

Here are some more syncopated parts created by the use of eighth rests on the beat.

DOUBLING NOTES IN CHORDS

The chords in the next two examples contain four notes. Because there are only three different notes in a major chord, this means that some of the notes are **doubled**. The most commonly doubled notes are the **root** and the **fifth**. Playing four note voicings requires a greater stretch between the fingers, so be patient and practice the chords by themselves at first.

37.1 Country Accompaniment

Here is a simple Country progression using four note chord voicings lower down on the keyboard. When you are accompanying other musicians, the pitch at which you choose to play largely depends on what the singer or other musicians are playing. Every instrument and voice has its most comfortable range or **register**. When playing with others, it is important not to clutter one register and leave too much space in others. As a keyboard player, you have more choice than singers or many other instrumentalists, so it is up to you to judge which register sounds best for your particular part. Always think of what will serve the overall sound best.

LESSON FIFTEEN

MINOR CHORD INVERSIONS

A MINOR CHORD INVERSIONS

These three diagrams illustrate the root position (1 ♭3 5), first inversion (♭3 5 1), and second inversion (5 1 ♭3) of the **Am** chord.

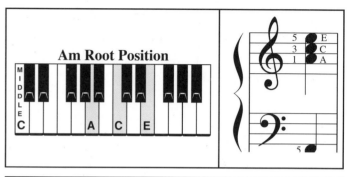

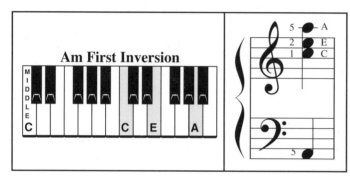

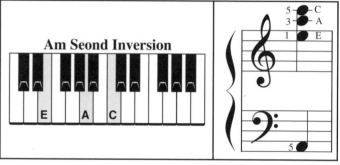

The following example uses the root position, first inversion, second inversion, and an octave of the root position of the **Am** chord. Use the fingerings shown in the diagrams.

 **38.0**

 **38.1**

Here is a keyboard part making use of all three inversions of the A minor chord. Notice the interplay between the two hands in this part.

SLASH CHORDS

The following examples make use of another important keyboard technique: i.e. playing a chord with the right hand over a specific bass note. Sometimes this note is different to the notes contained within the chord. In the example below, the symbol **G/E** occurs. This indicates a **G chord** played over an **E bass note**. This is called a **slash chord**. Slash chords can create many different harmonic effects. Each combination has a specific name and often creates an entirely new chord. This will be discussed more later in the book. Basically you can play any chord over any bass note as long as it sounds good. Experiment with playing all the chords you have learnt over various bass notes from the C major scale.

39.0

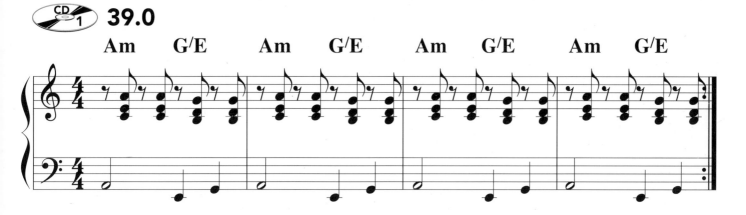

39.1

39.2

In this example the chords are played as arpeggios.

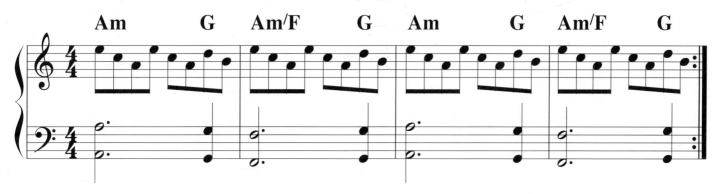

TURNAROUND PROGRESSIONS

A **Turnaround** progression is a set pattern of chords that repeats itself. There are hundreds of well known songs based on turnaround progressions. All these songs contain basically the same chords in the same order. A Turnaround may repeat over any number of bars. Usually 2, 4 and 8 bars. However the **chord sequence** remains the same. Most Turnarounds contain at least one minor chord. The following turnarounds contain the chords **C**, **Am**, **F** and **G**.

40.0

ACCENTS

An important expressive technique on any instrument is the use of **Accents**. An accent marking tells you to play the note louder than other notes. There are two common types of accents, which are shown below. The **long accent** is indicated by a **horizontal** wedge mark above or below the note. The **short accent** is indicated by a **vertical** wedge mark. Listen to the following example on the CD to hear the effect of accents.

Long accent   **Short Accent**

40.1

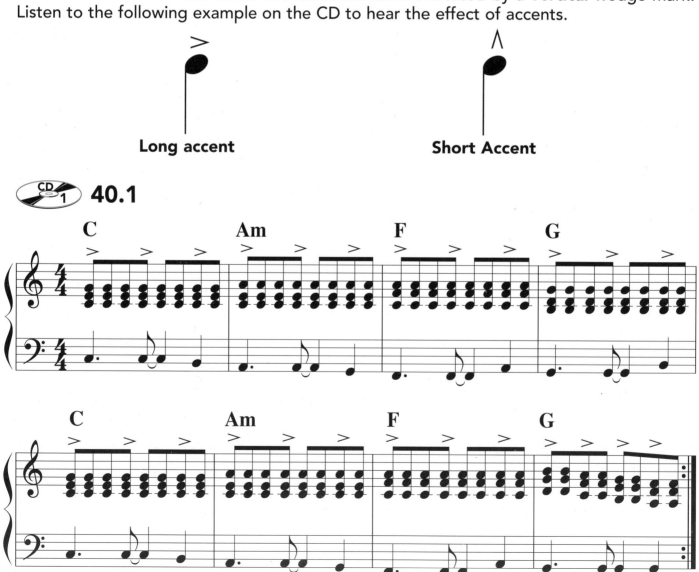

Here are some more examples which use accents. They are all turnaround progressions played in different positions on the keyboard.

 **40.2**

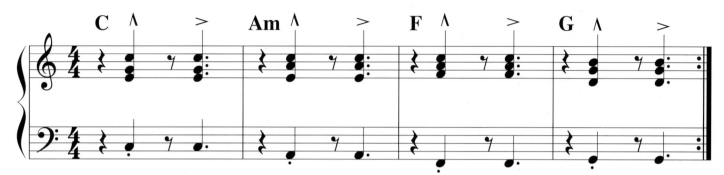

 **40.3**

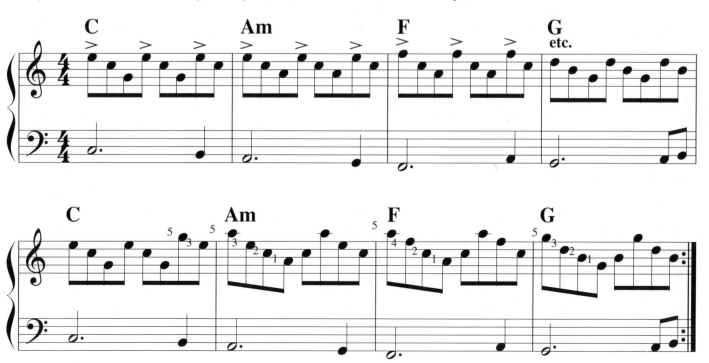 **40.4**

This one contains a repeated note pattern which results in a built–in accented rhythm. Experiment with this type of playing to create your own parts.

D MINOR CHORD INVERSIONS

These three diagrams illustrate the root position (1 ♭3 5), first inversion (♭3 5 1), and second inversion (5 1 ♭3) of the **Dm** chord.

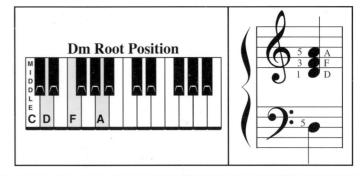

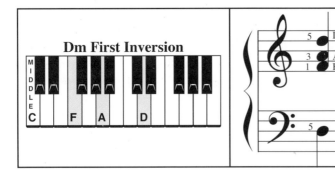

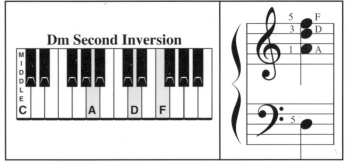

E MINOR CHORD INVERSIONS

These three diagrams illustrate the root position (1 ♭3 5), first inversion (♭3 5 1), and second inversion (5 1 ♭3) of the **Em** chord.

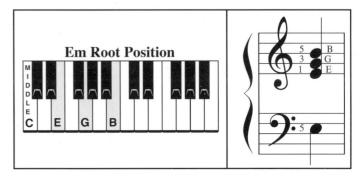

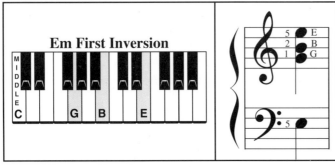

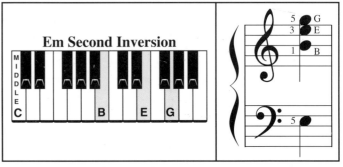

The following example uses all three inversions of the chords **D minor** and **E minor**.

41.0

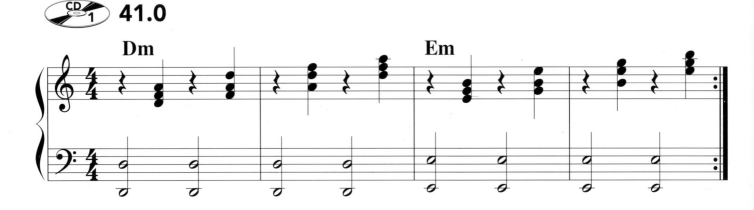

The following examples are common variations on the basic Turnaround progression. These examples all use the chords **Dm** and **Em**. Once you have them under your fingers, try playing the chords as arpeggios and experimenting with different inversions and different rhythms

41.1

41.2

41.3

LESSON SIXTEEN

MORE ABOUT SYNCOPATION

The use of **ties** is a common way of creating syncopated rhythms. The following example contains two bars of music using an Am chord. The first bar contains a rhythm of four eighth notes followed by a half note. In the second bar, the last eighth note is tied to the half note. Listen to the difference this makes to the rhythm. The use of ties in this manner is sometimes described as giving the rhythm a **push**.

42.0

Experiment with groups of eighth notes and ties in various parts of the bar as shown in the following examples.

42.1

42.2

42.3

Using a **push** is common between the last note of one bar and the first of the next bar.

IDENTIFYING EIGHTH NOTE RHYTHMS

There is a simple system for identifying any note's position in a bar by naming notes off the beat according to which beat they come directly after. The system works as follows. Within a bar of continuous eighth notes in $\frac{4}{4}$ time, there are **eight** possible places where notes could occur. The first beat is called **one** (1), the next eighth note is called the "**and of one**", then comes beat **two**, the next eighth note is called the "**and of two**", then beat **three**, followed by the "**and of three**", then beat **four**, followed by the "**and of four**" which is the final eighth note in the bar. These positions are shown in the notation below.

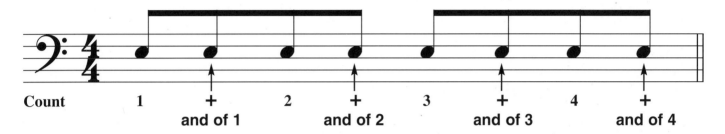

This system is particularly useful if you are having trouble with the timing of a rhythm. You simply identify where the notes occur in relation to each beat and then count them slowly until you have memorized the rhythm. Here is how the system can be used to analyze rhythms. In the right hand part of the following example, the chords are played on **2**, the **+ of 3** and the **+ of 4** in the first bar, and the last note in the bar is tied to a whole note which is held for the length of the second bar. The whole rhythm then repeats every two bars. Try analyzing the left hand part in this manner and write the count between the staves if necessary. Use this method every time you have trouble with a rhythm.

43.0

PEDAL TONES

This example once again uses slash chords. This time, all three chords are played over the one bass note. When moving chords are used over a bass note, the bass note is described as a **pedal tone**, or **pedal note**. Pedal tones occur in many different styles of music and were extensively used by classical composers. This piece features a rhythm using dotted quarter notes and ties. It is called a **Charleston rhythm**, which is common in Rock, Jazz and Blues. analyze it using the system shown on the previous page and count out loud as you play.

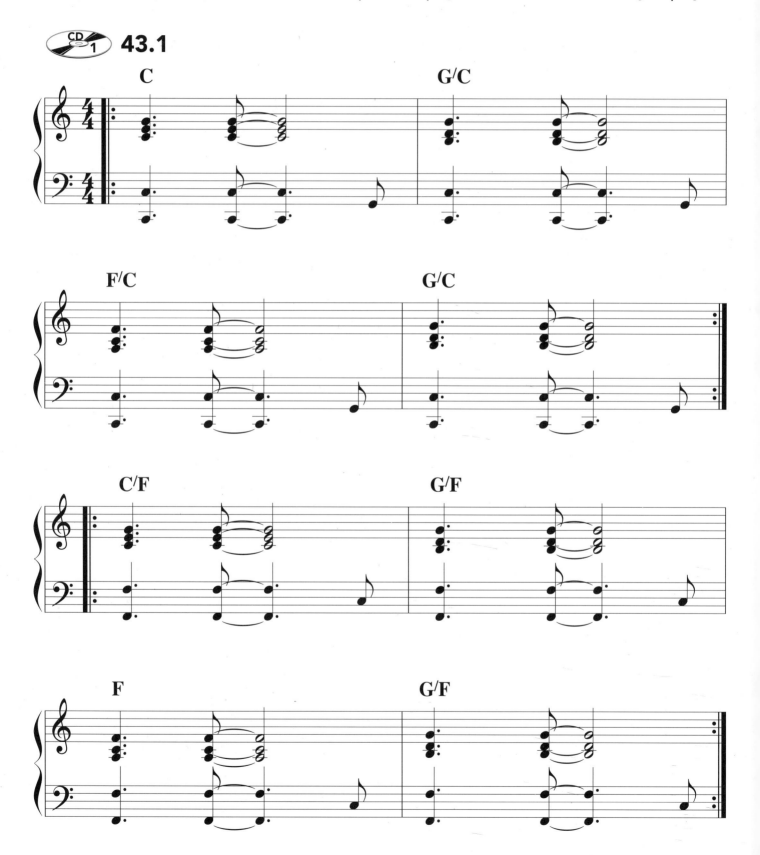

LESSON SEVENTEEN

THE SIXTEENTH NOTE

This is a **sixteenth note**.
It lasts for **one quarter** of a beat.
There are **four** sixteenth notes in one beat.
There are **16** sixteenth notes in one bar of 4/4 time.

Two sixteenth notes joined together.

Four sixteenth notes joined together.

Count: 1   e   +   a
Say: one 'ee' and 'ah'

44.0 How to Count 16th Notes

When counting 16th notes, notice the different sound for each part of the beat – **one ee and ah**, **two ee and ah**... etc (written **1 e + a, 2 e + a**... etc).

44.1

As with any new note value, it is important to practice your scales using 16th notes until you are comfortable with them. Here is the **C major scale** played in sixteenth notes over four octaves. Take it slowly at first, and remember to use your metronome and count out loud as you play.

45. Arkansas Traveller

This traditional American folk song features several 16th note passages. Although many of the eighth notes are played staccato, all the **16th notes** should be played **legato**. Practice each hand separately until you are comfortable with both parts and then put them together. If you have trouble co-ordinating the two hands, practice one bar at a time very slowly and only increase the speed when you can play the whole piece.

Allegro

DYNAMICS

The term **dynamics** refers to the **volume** at which music is played. If all music was played at the same volume it would lack expression and soon become boring. Therefore it is necessary to be able to play at a variety of dynamic levels ranging from very soft to very loud. There are various markings for dynamics in written music. Most come from Italian words. Some of these are listed below, along with their English translations. To practice dynamics, play a scale, and then a melody at each of these volumes.

pp   pianissimo (very soft)

p   piano (soft)

mp   mezzo piano (moderately soft)

mf   mezzo forte (moderately loud)

f   forte (loud)

ff   fortissimo (very loud)

VOLUME CHANGES

crescendo   diminuendo

Gradual changes in volume are indicated by the **crescendo** (meaning a gradual increase in volume) and the **diminuendo** (meaning a gradual decrease in volume). Listen to the way they are applied to the scale in the following example.

CD 1   **46.0**

Learning to use dynamics effectively takes quite a while. A good way to practice dynamics is to play a basic rhythm (e.g two bars of eighth notes) on one note, but at different dynamic levels, ranging from as softly as you can play to as loudly as you can play. Then try the same thing with a short melody. These two extremes are not so difficult, although keeping all the notes consistent when playing very quietly can be tricky at first. Most beginners have trouble making the grades of volume in between *pp* and *f* distinguishable, so be patient and keep practicing until you are comfortable with all the dynamic levels shown above.

Once you are comfortable with different dynamic levels, start adding crescendos and diminuendos. Again, start with one note until you are comfortable with gradual and consistent volume changes, then try crescendos and diminuendos with scales and finally with melodies. An instrumentalist with good control of dynamics and time will always be in demand with other musicians and well appreciated by audiences.

46.1 Czerny 16th Note Study

Here is a sixteenth note study by **Czerny**. It contains several dynamic markings including a crescendo over two bars. The way you use dynamics can make a huge difference to the feeling of the music and the response it evokes in a listener.

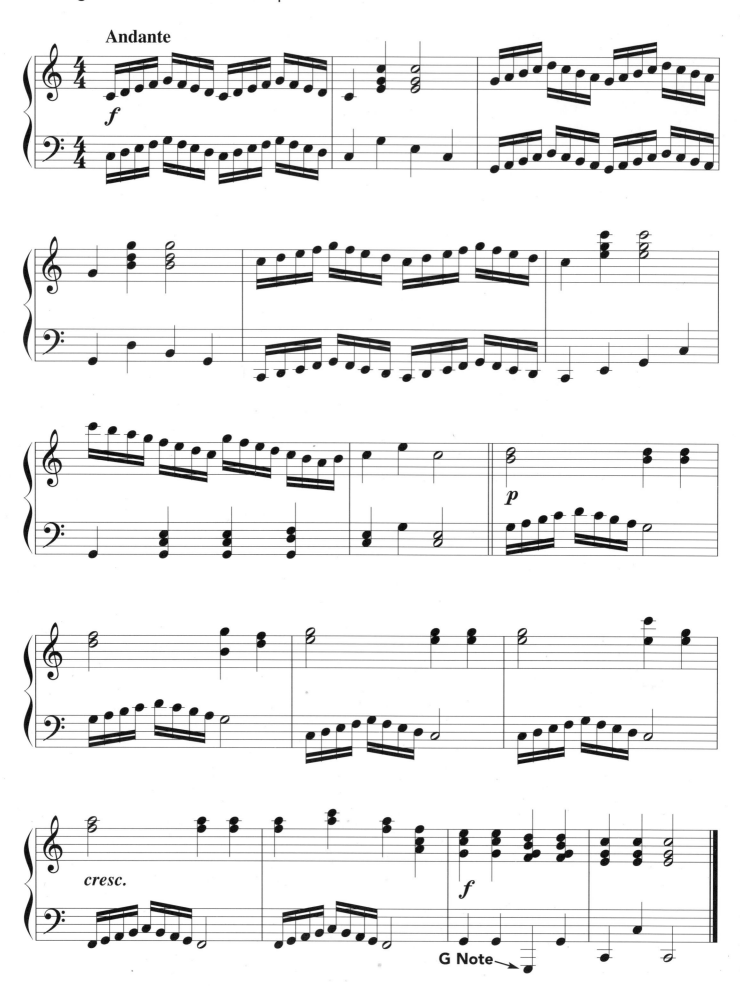

LESSON EIGHTEEN

ACCIDENTALS

Sometimes it is necessary to use notes which are not within the key signature of a piece of music. This is when **accidentals** are used. An accidental is a temporary alteration to the pitch of a note. An accidental may be a sharp, a flat, or a natural. A **natural sign** (shown below) is used to cancel a sharp or flat. Like a sharp of flat, the natural affects all notes of that pitch for the rest of the bar in which it occurs, unless another accidental occurs after it.

 THE NATURAL SIGN.

 **47.0**

This example demonstrates accidentals applied to the note **G** in the treble staff. Notice that **G♭** is the same note as **F♯** which you already know.

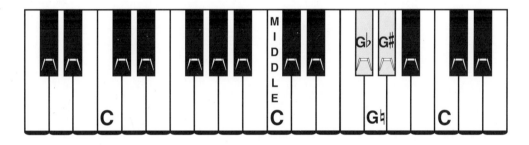

ENHARMONIC NOTES

As you saw in the previous example, the note **G♭** is exactly the same as **F♯**. In music there is often more than one way of naming a note, e.g. **D♯** is the same note as **E♭**, **B♭** is the same note as **A♯**, etc. The different names are called **enharmonic** notes. All the black notes on the keyboard have more than one name, and white notes can as well, e.g. **E♮** is also **F♭**, and **F♮** is also **E♯**.

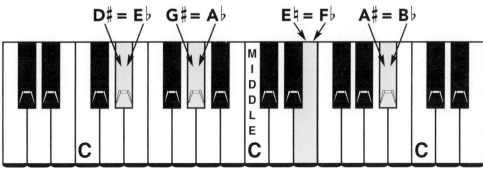

12 BAR BLUES

The following piece is an example of the **12 bar Blues** – a musical form central to the **African American** music tradition. It uses a pattern of chords that repeats every 12 bars and may be played in any key. This one contains many accidentals, so take it slowly at first to be sure you are playing the correct notes. Whenever you are learning a melody which contains new notes, play slowly and sing the names of all the notes out loud as you play. Listen carefully as you do this, and try to sing the same pitch as you are playing.

47.1   Accidental Blues

THE CHROMATIC SCALE

With the inclusion of sharps and flats, there are 12 different notes within one octave as shown below. The notes **E to F** and **B to C** are always one **semitone** apart. A semitone is the smallest possible distance between two notes. All the other natural notes are a **tone** apart (two semitones). Sharps (♯) and flats (♭) are found between the notes that are a tone apart:

This is called the **chromatic scale**. It contains all the sharps (♯'s) and flats (♭'s) possible between one C note and its repeat an octave higher or lower. All the **black** notes have **two** names (enharmonic spellings). **C sharp** (C♯) has the same position on the keyboard as **D flat** (D♭). They are the same note but can have different names depending on what key you are playing in. The same applies to D♯ /E♭, F♯ /G♭, G♯ /A♭ and A♯ /B♭.

48   C Chromatic Scale

By learning the chromatic scale, you will become more familiar with all the black notes . Many beginners think they are harder to play because their names contain sharps and flats, but they are just as easy to play as the white notes and are essential for playing in keys other than C major. Notice that only **three** fingers are required to play the chromatic scale. Once you memorize the fingering, the scale is simple to play.

DOTTED EIGHTH NOTES

As you know, a dot after a note increases its value by half. Thus a dotted eighth note is equal to three sixteenth notes, as shown below. The dotted eighth note is often followed by a sixteenth note. Together they add up to one beat.

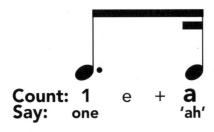

Count: 1   e   +   **a**
Say: one   'ah'

The dotted eighth note is equivalent to the duration of three sixteenth notes.

 **49.0**

The following example demonstrates the use of dotted eighth notes. Count out loud as you play, and be sure to keep the rhythms of the two hands independent.

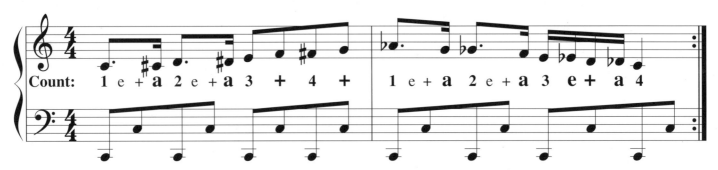

Sometimes you will find the figure reversed, i.e. a sixteenth note followed by a dotted eighth note, as shown below.

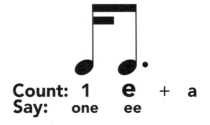

Count: 1   **e**   +   a
Say: one   ee

 **49.1**

Listen to the CD to hear the effect produced by this rhythm. Once again Count out loud as you play.

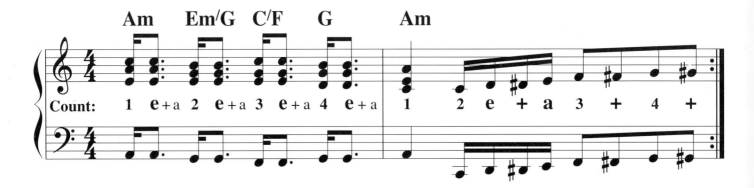

50. Dungeons and Dragons

This piece uses both of the dotted eighth note rhythms you have just learned. It features a simple one beat left hand part which is is repeated throughout. Using one note or chord under moving parts is called a **drone**. This technique is common in folk music and medieval music. The right hand part is quite tricky, so be patient with it and learn it one bar at a time if you need to.

LESSON NINETEEN

VOICE PARTS

If you listen to a group of musicians playing together, you will notice that there are times when one person plays a sustained note or chord while another plays a moving part. Because the keyboard is capable of playing many notes at the same time, this same musical technique can be used by one keyboard player. When you have one note sustained with a moving part over or under it, the lines are written as individual **voice parts**, with the note stems going in different directions. This originally comes from choral music, where a chord is made up of three or more notes sung by human voices. The following example is a simple demonstration of voice parts, containing a moving voice in the middle part.

51.0 **(Organ Sound)**

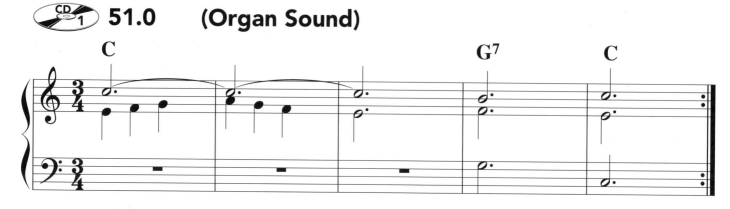

51.1

When playing music containing individual voice parts, it is often necessary to sustain a note by keeping a key pressed down while playing other notes with other fingers on the same hand. This can be difficult at first, and requires a great deal of slow, concentrated practice before it becomes automatic. Here is an exercise to help you develop this technique.

51.2

One of the simplest uses of voice parts is a sustained bass note at the beginning of each bar, with an inner rhythmic part played by other fingers of the left hand on the remaining beats of the bar. In this example, the technique is used to provide a waltz accompaniment.

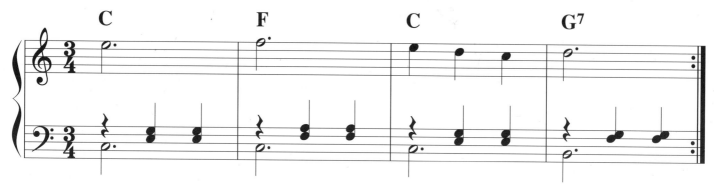

52. Czerny Study

Here is a study by Czerny which uses the same technique in 4/4 time. All the bass notes are played by the 5th finger of the left hand. Be sure to hold each one till the end of the bar, so that it keeps sustaining under the chords played by the other fingers of the left hand. Notice that both hands are reading treble clef in this piece.

CUT COMMON TIME

The following piece features a new time signature which is a variation on the Common time symbol, but this one has a vertical line through it ₵. This is called **cut common time**, or simply cut time. It is also called $\frac{2}{2}$ time and represents two half note beats per bar. In this situation, each half note receives one count. Whole notes receive two counts, while quarter notes receive half a count. This is a traditional church melody arranged as a **chorale** (choir or **choral** style piece) by 19th century composer **Robert Schumann**. The chords are made up of **four individual voice parts** - two played by each hand. it also features the **fermata** or pause sign ⌢, which is used to indicate that a note or chord is held at the player's own discretion.

53. **Chorale**

R Schumann

LESSON TWENTY

USING THE SUSTAIN PEDAL

When moving between chords, it is often necessary to lift one or both hands off the keyboard completely. This results in a gap in sound between one chord and the next. Sometimes this is desirable, and other times it is not. The use of the **sustain pedal** makes it possible to keep a note or chord sounding while the hands move to a new position.

On a piano, the pedal is part of the instrument itself. There are also other pedals on the piano which vary between upright and grand pianos. For now, we will deal specifically with the sustain pedal. The sustain pedal (also called the **sostenuto** pedal) is always the one to the **right** of the other pedals, because it is operated with the **right foot**. On electronic keyboards the sustain pedal is a separate attachment which can be plugged into the socket provided on the back of the keyboard.

The photos below show the pedals on both upright and grand pianos as well as a sustain pedal for an electronic keyboard. To hear how the sustain pedal works, play a chord and then press the pedal down with your right foot. Hold the pedal down and lift your hands off the keyboard - the chord keeps sounding as long as the pedal is held down. This makes changing chords a lot easier.

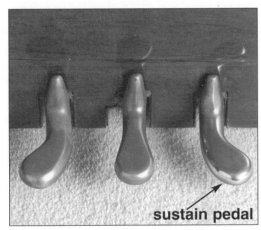

Upright Piano Pedals

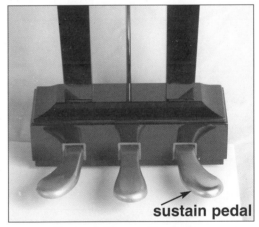

Grand Piano Pedals

Electronic Keyboard Pedal

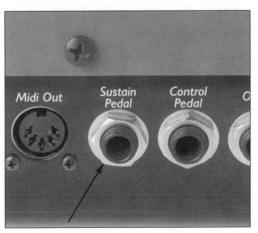

Socket on Back of Keyboard

The following example demonstrates a typical use of the sustain pedal. In the first two bars, the right hand moves between inversions of a C major chord. Listen to the gap between each chord as the hand is lifted off the keyboard. In the third and fourth bars, the sustain pedal is pressed down as each new inversion is played. This eliminates the gaps in sound between the chords. The use of the pedal is indicated by the symbol **Ped.**

54.0

The basic rule when using the sustain pedal is that it must be **released when the harmony changes**. This is demonstrated in the following example. The pedal is held down between bars 1 and 2 while the left hand changes from a **C** chord to a **G7** chord. When the pedal is held down, the first chord blends in with the second chord, causing a clash in harmony and a muddy sound. This is definitely undesirable! In the rest of the example, **the pedal is quickly released as each new chord is struck by the hand and then immediately pressed down again until the next chord is struck**. This is the correct way to use the pedal. Practice this example many times each day until you can co-ordinate it with your hand. Then try playing the chords with the right hand, then both hands.

54.1

55.

In this example, broken chords are played by the right hand. Because each all the notes are part of the one harmony, it is not necessary to release the pedal until a new chord is played.

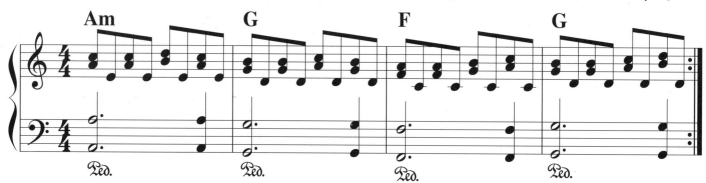

56. Aloha Oe

This traditional Pacific song contains much movement between chord inversions, making it an excellent study for pedalling. Follow the pedal indications and remember the basic principle is that the pedal is released and depressed again each time the harmony changes.

Once you can play this piece, go back to the **Chorale** on page 84 and play it with the pedal.

LESSON TWENTY ONE

SCALE TONE CHORDS

The example below shows chords built on all the degrees of the **C** major scale. In **any** key it is possible to build chords on each degree of the scale. This means that for every major scale there are **seven** possible chords which can be used for creating keyboard parts and harmonizing melodies created from that scale. These seven chords are called **scale tone chords**. It is common practice to describe chords within a key with **roman numerals** as shown here.

 **57.0**

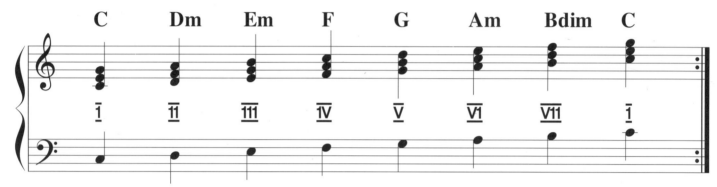

The **B diminished** chord contains the notes **B**, **D** and **F**. Like major and minor chords it can be played in three inversions which are shown below.

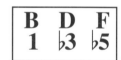

Chord Symbol

Bdim
or
B°

1 ♭3 5

THE B DIMINISHED CHORD

Notes in Chord

B	D	F
1	♭3	♭5

B DIMINISHED CHORD INVERSIONS

These three diagrams illustrate the root position (1 ♭3 ♭5), first inversion (♭3 ♭5 1), and second inversion (♭5 1 ♭3) of the **Bdim** chord.

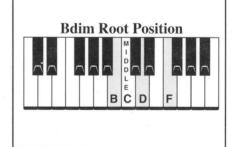

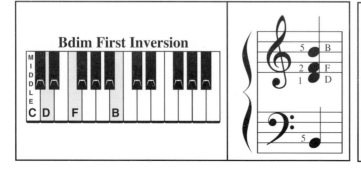

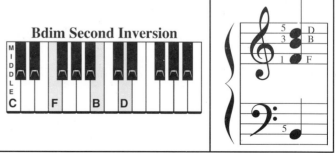

Example 57.1 demonstrates the root position, first inversion, second inversion, and an octave of the root position of the Bdim chord.

 57.1

USING ROMAN NUMERALS FOR CHORDS

If you look at some simple progressions in the key of C major, it is easy to see how the system of roman numerals works. The following example contains the chords **C**, **F** and **G**. Since these chords correspond to the first, fourth and fifth degrees of the C major scale, the progression could be described as Ī ĪV V̄ Ī in the **key of C**.

58.0

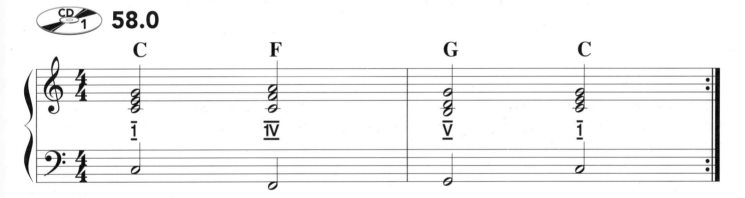

 **58.1**

This one contains the chords **C**, **Em**, **Dm** and **G** which correspond to the first, third, second and fifth degrees of the C major scale: therefore the progression could be described as Ī ĪĪĪ ĪĪ V̄ in the key of C.

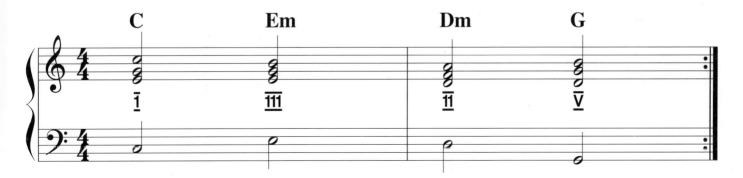

Even when you see a more complex keyboard part, it is usually based on a simple underlying chord progression. Try reducing the following examples to block chords, then try taking any progression and making a keyboard part out of it by using broken chords, arpeggios, adding notes to the chords and varying the rhythm.

**59.**

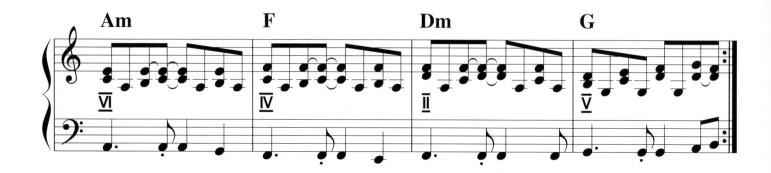

**60.**

This part looks more complex and is harder to play, but it is based on an even simpler underlying chord progression. Analyze the progression underlying everything you learn and experiment with different ways of playing it.

PASSING NOTES

The following organ style piece uses voice parts containing a combination of chords and connecting scale runs. In these runs, the notes on the beat are usually chord tones, while the notes between the beats are non chord tones. These are called **passing notes**.

61.

Here is a piece which uses all the scale tone chords in the key of **C**. Notice the use of slash chords and passing notes throughout the piece. Don't forget to experiment with using the sustain pedal. Most sheet music doesn't contain pedal markings, as it is left to the player's discretion. The general principle is that the busier the part is rhythmically, the less the pedal is used. No two players pedal exactly the same, so over time you need to develop a method that works best for you.

62. Seven Seas

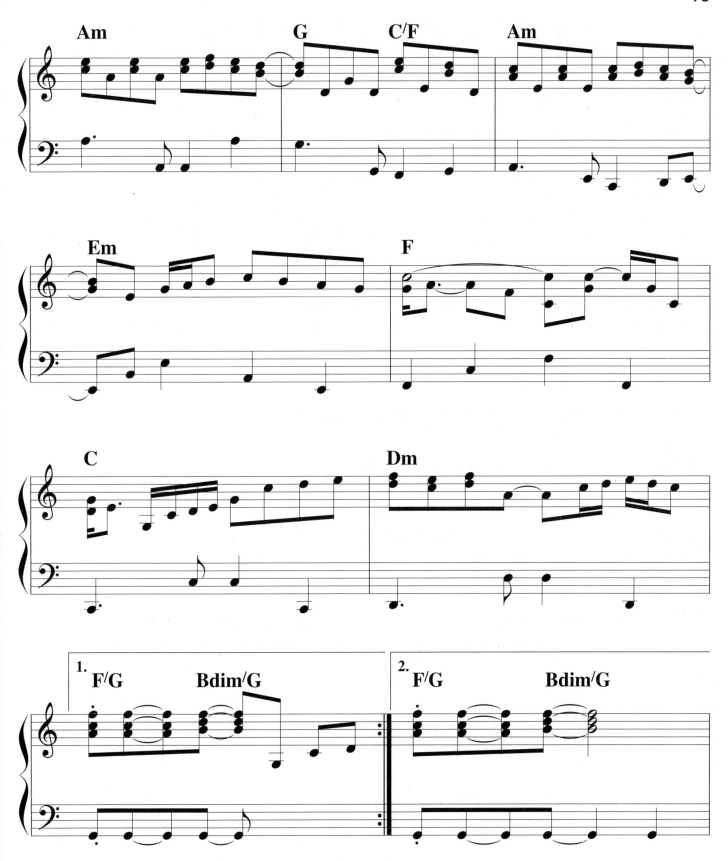

LESSON TWENTY TWO

INTERVALS

An interval is the distance between two musical notes. Intervals are measured in numbers, and are calculated by counting the number of letter names (**A B C D E F G A**) between and including the notes being measured. Within an octave, intervals are: **Unison** (two notes of the same pitch played or sung together or consecutively), **2nd**, **3rd**, **4th**, **5th**, **6th**, **7th** and **Octave** (two notes an octave apart). Thus **A** to **B** is a **2nd** interval, as is B to C, C to D etc. **A** to **C** is a **3rd** interval, **A** to **D** is a **4th**, **A** to **E** is a **5th**, **A** to **F** is a **6th**, **A** to **G** is a **7th** and **A** to the next **A** is an **octave**.

Intervals may be **melodic** (two notes played consecutively) or **harmonic** (two notes played at the same time). Hence two people singing at the same time are said to be singing in harmony.

INTERVAL QUALITIES

Different intervals have different qualities, as shown below:

Quality	Can be applied to
Perfect	Unisons, 4ths, 5ths and Octaves
Major	2nds, 3rds, 6ths and 7ths
Minor	2nds, 3rds, 6ths and 7ths
Augmented	All intervals
Diminished	All intervals

These intervals can be best explained with the aid of a chromatic scale. If you look at the one below, it is easy to see that since intervals are measured in semitones, they may begin or end on a sharp or flat rather than a natural note.

$$A \quad {}^{A\sharp}\!/\!_{B\flat} \quad B \quad C \quad {}^{C\sharp}\!/\!_{D\flat} \quad D \quad {}^{D\sharp}\!/\!_{E\flat} \quad E \quad F \quad {}^{F\sharp}\!/\!_{G\flat} \quad G \quad {}^{G\sharp}\!/\!_{A\flat} \quad A$$

Perfect intervals are **4ths**, **5ths** and **octaves**. If you **widen** a perfect interval by a semitone it becomes **augmented** (added to). E.g. if you add a semitone to the perfect 4th interval **C** to **F**, it becomes the **augmented 4th interval C** to **F♯**. Notice that the letter name remains the same–it is not referred to as C to G♭.

If you narrow a perfect interval by a semitone they become **diminished** (lessened). E.g. if you lessen the perfect 5th interval **D** to **A** by a semitone, it becomes the **diminished 5th interval D to A♭**. Again, the letter name remains the same–it is not referred to as D to G♯.

Major intervals (2nds, 3rds, 6ths and 7ths) become minor if narrowed by a semitone and **minor** intervals become major if widened by a semitone. A **diminished** interval can be created by narrowing a perfect or minor interval by a semitone. An **augmented** interval can be created by widening a perfect or major interval by a semitone.

INTERVAL DISTANCES

In summary, here is a list of the distances of all common intervals up to an octave measured in semitones. Each new interval is one semitone wider apart than the previous one. Notice that the interval of an octave is exactly twelve semitones. This is because there are twelve different notes in the chromatic scale. Notice also that the interval which has a distance of six semitones can be called either an augmented 4th or a diminished 5th. This interval is also often called a **tritone** (6 semitones = 3 tones).

Minor 2nd - One semitone

Major 2nd - Two semitones

Minor 3rd - Three semitones

Major 3rd - Four semitones

Perfect 4th - Five semitones

Augmented 4th or Diminished 5th - Six semitones

Perfect 5th - Seven semitones

Minor 6th - Eight semitones

Major 6th - Nine semitones

Minor 7th - Ten semitones

Major 7th - Eleven semitones

Perfect Octave - Twelve semitones

The following example demonstrates all of the common intervals ascending within one octave starting and ending on the note **C**.

63.

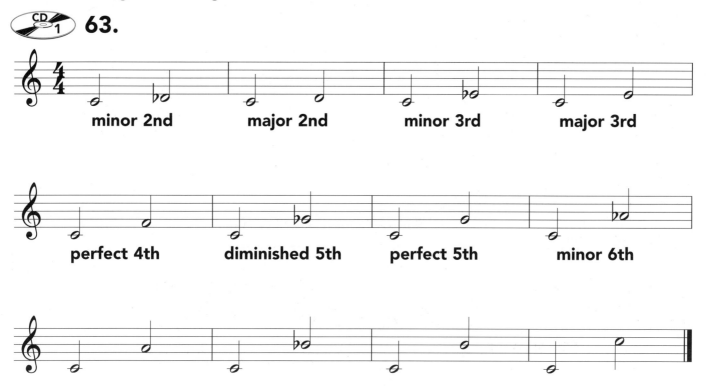

CHORD CONSTRUCTION

Chords are usually made up of combinations of major and minor third intervals. All of the chords you have learnt up to this point have been **triads** (3 note chords). There are **four** basic types of triads: **major**, **minor**, **augmented** and **diminished**. Examples of each of these triads are shown below along with the formula for each one.

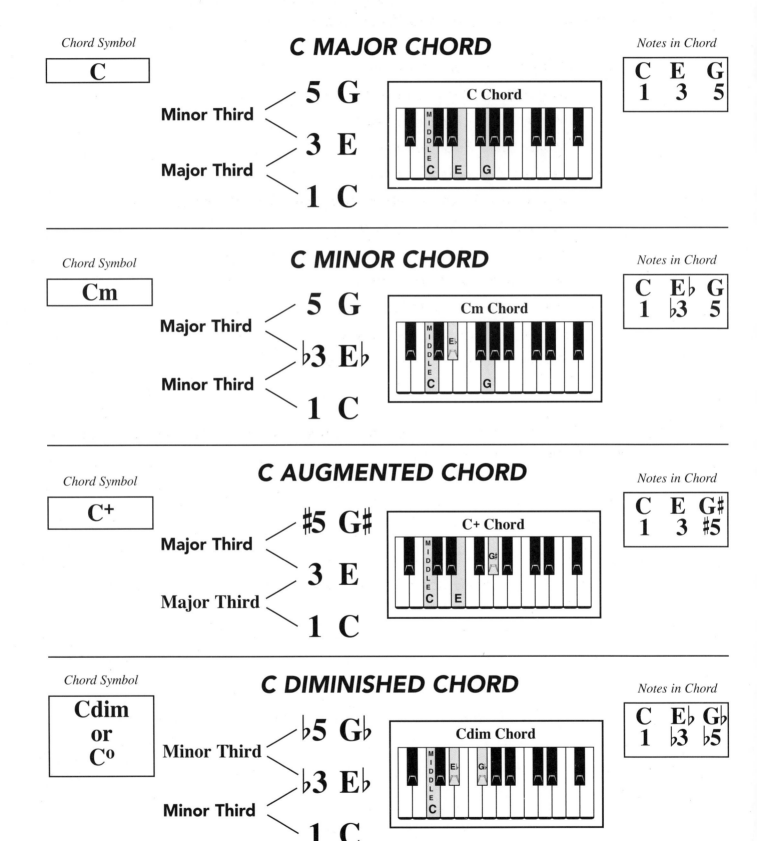

Chord Symbol

C MAJOR CHORD

Notes in Chord

C

C	E	G
1	3	5

Minor Third — 5 G
Major Third — 3 E
1 C

C Chord

Chord Symbol

C MINOR CHORD

Notes in Chord

Cm

C	E♭	G
1	♭3	5

Major Third — 5 G
Minor Third — ♭3 E♭
1 C

Cm Chord

Chord Symbol

C AUGMENTED CHORD

Notes in Chord

C+

C	E	G♯
1	3	♯5

Major Third — ♯5 G♯
Major Third — 3 E
1 C

C+ Chord

Chord Symbol

C DIMINISHED CHORD

Notes in Chord

Cdim
or
C°

C	E♭	G♭
1	♭3	♭5

Minor Third — ♭5 G♭
Minor Third — ♭3 E♭
1 C

Cdim Chord

This example demonstrates the four basic types of triads shown on the previous page.

 64.   The Four Basic Triad Types

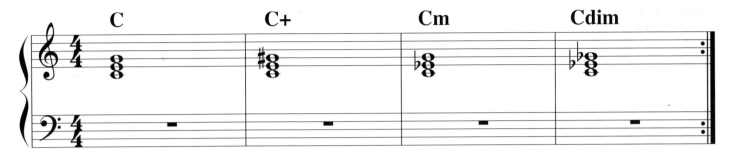

 65.

All types of chords can be played in different positions on the keyboard in various inversions. This example demonstrates how the four basic triad types could be used in a more musical manner. The right hand plays voicings which are close together on the keyboard, while the left hand outlines each chord as an arpeggio starting from the root.

SCALE TONE CHORDS IN G

By using the correct formulas, it is possible to build any of the four types of triads on any note of the chromatic scale. E.g. if you start with the note D and add a note a major third above it (F♯) and a minor third above that (A) you end up with a D major chord. If you start with the note A and add a note a minor third above it (C) and a major third above that (E) you end up with an A minor chord.

If you go through and analyse all of the scale tone chords in the key of C major you end up with the following pattern:

I̲	Major	(C Major)
I̲I̲	Minor	(D Minor)
I̲I̲I̲	Minor	(E Minor)
I̲V̲	Major	(F Major)
V̲	Major	(G Major)
V̲I̲	Minor	(A Minor)
V̲I̲I̲	Diminished	(B Diminished)

This pattern remains the same regardless of the key. This means that if you look at the scale tone triads in **any major key**, Chord I̲ is **always** major, chord I̲I̲ is always minor, chord I̲I̲I̲ is always minor, etc. The only thing that changes from one key to the next is the letter names of the chords. This can be demonstrated by looking at the scale tone triads for the key of **G major** which are shown below.

 **66.**

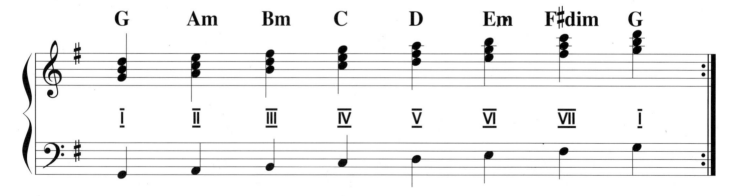

LESSON TWENTY THREE

HOW TO TRANSPOSE

Transposing (or transposition) means changing the key of a piece of music. By using the system of roman numerals it is very easy to transpose a chord progression from one key to another. The same system is also useful for communicating progressions and parts to other musicians.

The example below shows a simple keyboard part in the key of C, based on the chords C. F and G. This progression can be described as Ī IV̄ V̄.

67.0

67.1

To transpose the above part to the key of G, you need to know chords Ī IV̄ V̄ in that key (G, C and D). Here is the same part transposed to the key of G.

NEW CHORDS IN THE KEY OF G

The above example contains the chord **D major** which you have not previously learnt. By using the chord construction formulas from the previous lesson you can easily work out that a **D chord** contains the notes **D, F♯** and **A**. Like any chord, there is more than one way to play a D chord. The diagrams on the following page show the D chord in root position, first inversion and second inversion.

D MAJOR CHORD INVERSIONS

These three diagrams illustrate the root position (1 3 5), first inversion (3 5 1), and second inversion (5 1 3) of the **D** chord.

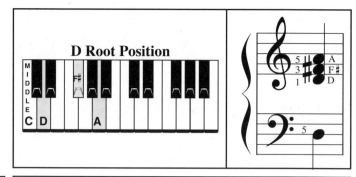

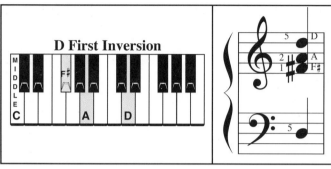

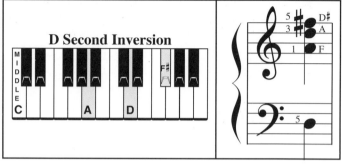

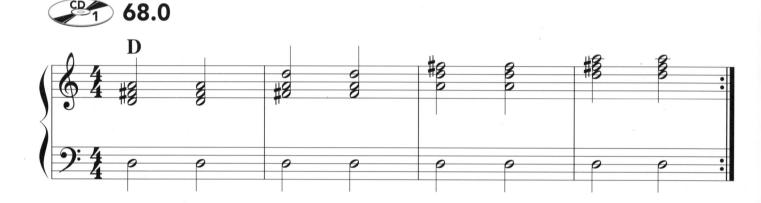

The key of G also contains the chords **B minor** and **F# diminished**. In the following diagrams, these chords are shown in root position, first inversion and second inversion.

B MINOR CHORD INVERSIONS

These three diagrams illustrate the root position (1 ♭3 5), first inversion (♭3 5 1), and second inversion (5 1 ♭3) of the **Bm** chord.

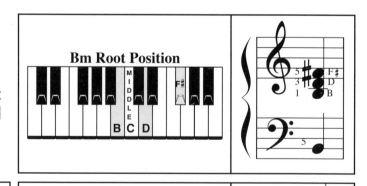

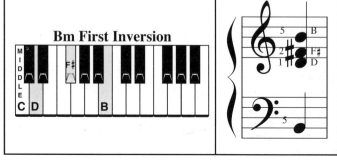

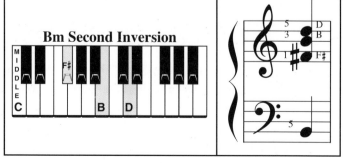

 **68.1**

This example contains all three inversions of the **Bm** chord.

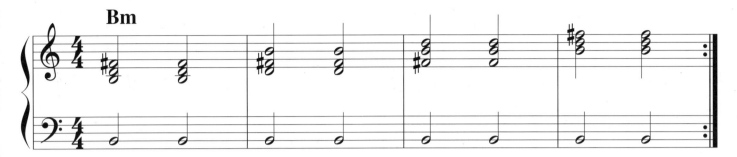

F♯ DIMINISHED CHORD INVERSIONS

These three diagrams illustrate the root position (1 ♭3 ♭5), first inversion (♭3 ♭5 1), and second inversion (♭5 1 ♭3) of the **F♯** dim chord.

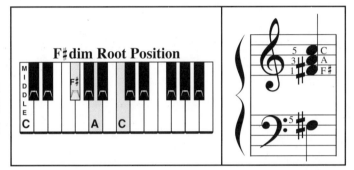

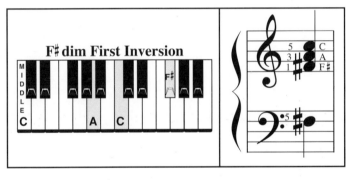

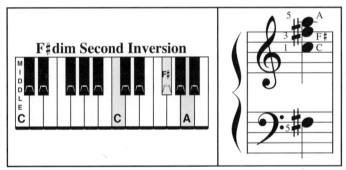

 **68.2**

 **69.**

Here is a keyboard part which makes use of the chords **Bm** and **F♯** dim.

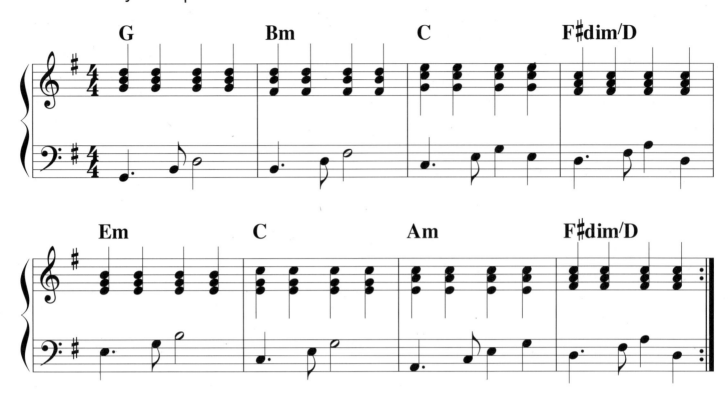

 **70.**

Like any piece of music, the above example can be transposed to other keys. Here is the same part in the key of **C**.

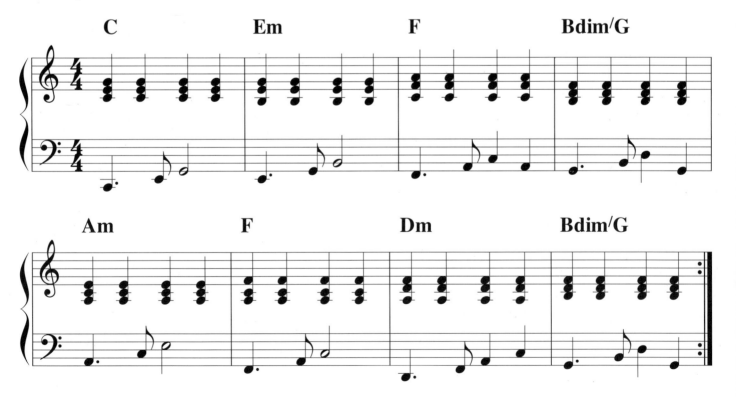

LESSON TWENTY FOUR

MINOR SCALES AND KEYS

Apart from major keys, the other basic tonality used in western music is a **minor key**. Minor keys are often said to have a sadder or darker sound than major keys. Songs in a minor key use notes taken from a **minor scale**. There are three types of minor scale – the **natural minor scale**, the **harmonic minor scale** and the **melodic minor scale**. Written below is the **A natural minor** scale. It contains exactly the same notes as the C major scale. The difference is that it starts and finishes on an **A** note instead of a C note. The A note then becomes the key note. The A natural minor scale is easy to learn – it is simply the notes of the **musical alphabet**.

A Natural Minor Scale	A	B	C	D	E	F	G	A
C Major Scale	C	D	E	F	G	A	B	C

71. A Natural Minor Scale

Here is the A natural minor scale played with both hands – first in eighth notes over two octaves and then in sixteenth notes over three octaves.

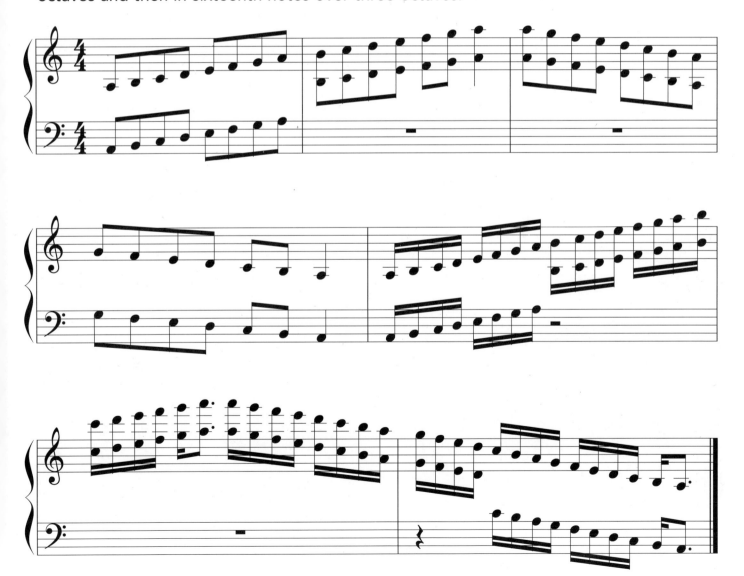

TEMPO CHANGES

There are specific markings for changes in tempo. The most common ones are listed below. Notice the use of the **rit** marking near the end of the following song.

accelerando (gradually becoming faster)

rallentando
or
ritardando
(gradually becoming slower)

ritenuto (**rit**) (immediately slower)

a tempo (return to the original tempo)

72.   God Rest Ye Merry Gentlemen

The melody of this traditional christmas song is derived from the natural minor scale. Because of this, it is said to be in a **minor key**. It is written here in the key of **A minor**.

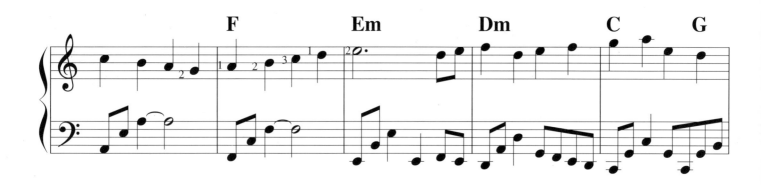

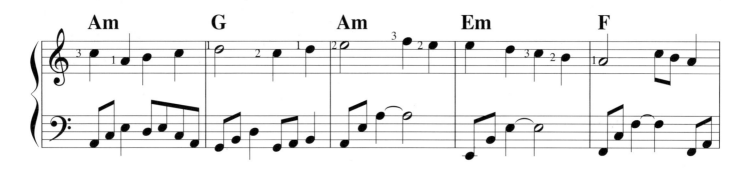

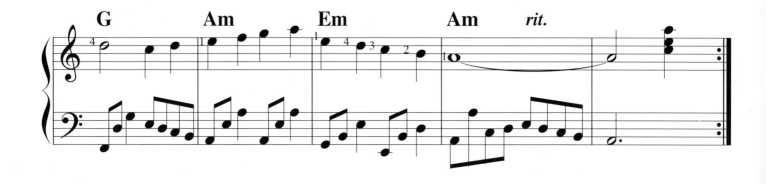

RELATIVE MAJOR AND MINOR KEYS

Look at the song on the previous page, and notice that although the previous piece is in the key of **A minor**, all the chords it contains are also in the key of C major. For every key signature there are two possible keys, one major and one minor. These are called **relative** keys, e.g. the key signature for the key of C major contains **no sharps or flats**, as does the key of A minor. The key of A minor is therefore called the **relative minor** of C major.

 The key signatures for **C Major** and **A minor** are identical - no sharps or flats.

To find the relative minor of any major key, start on the 6th degree of the major scale. The example below shows the scale tone chords for the key of A natural minor. Notice that the chords are exactly the same as those contained in the key of C major. The only difference is the starting and finishing point. Because the minor scale starts on **A**, A minor will now be chord $\overline{\text{I}}$ instead of $\overline{\text{VI}}$.

 **73.**

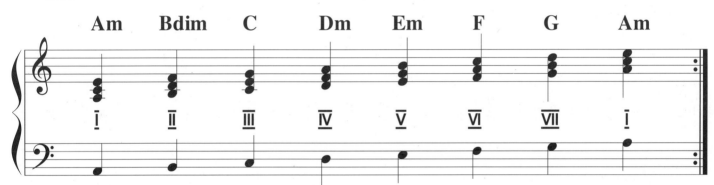

The following progression could be described in two possible ways. It could be called $\overline{\text{VI}}$ $\overline{\text{V}}$ $\overline{\text{VI}}$ $\overline{\text{IV}}$ $\overline{\text{V}}$ in **C major** or $\overline{\text{I}}$ $\overline{\text{VII}}$ $\overline{\text{I}}$ $\overline{\text{VI}}$ $\overline{\text{VII}}$ in **A minor**. Because the progression has an obvious minor sounding tonality, musicians would use the second description. Experiment with other chord combinations in the key of A minor.

 **74.**

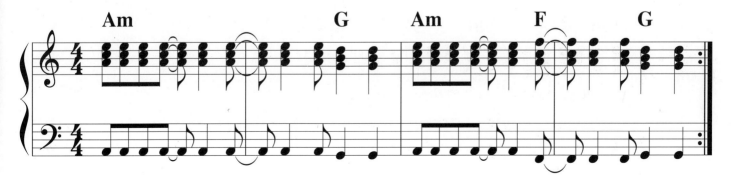

Written below are the scale tone chords for the key of **E natural minor** which is the relative minor of **G** major, as shown by the key signature. As with the keys of C major and A minor, the chords will be the same as those of its relative, but the starting note is **E** instead of G, so **E minor** will be chord Ī.

75.

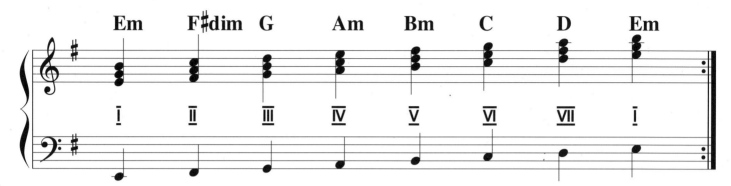

Like music written in major keys, anything in a minor key can be transposed to other keys. The following example shows the keyboard part from example 74 transposed to the key of **E minor**.

76.

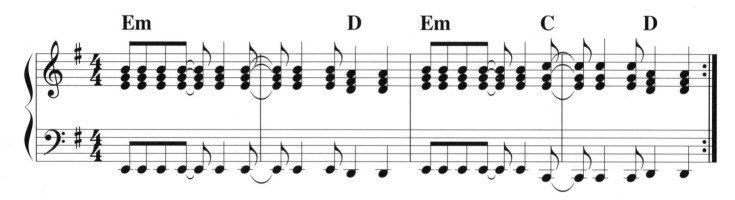

77.

Sometimes only two chords are needed to give the effect of a minor key. Notice also the use of space in this keyboard part. Particularly when playing with other instruments, it is not necessary to play all the time. Try transposing this part to the key of A minor.

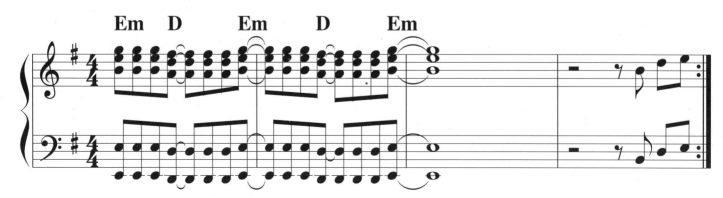

LESSON TWENTY FIVE

MORE ABOUT MINOR KEYS AND SCALES

For every minor key, there are three basic types of minor scale—the **natural minor scale**, the **harmonic minor scale** and the **melodic minor scale**. Each has its own pattern of tones and semitones, as can be seen in the three A minor scales below. The degrees of each scale are written under the note names.

 78.0 A Natural Minor

T	S	T	T	S	T	T

A	B	C	D	E	F	G	A
1	2	♭3	4	5	♭6	♭7	1

 78.1 A Harmonic Minor

Notice the distance of 1½ tones (three semitones) between the 6th and 7th degrees of the harmonic minor scale. This scale is often described as having an "Eastern" sound.

T	S	T	T	S	T1½	T

A	B	C	D	E	F	G♯	A
1	2	♭3	4	5	♭6	7	1

 **78.2 A Melodic Minor**

In the **A melodic minor** scale the **6th** and **7th** notes are sharpened when ascending and return to natural when descending. This is the way the melodic minor is used in Classical music. However, in Jazz and other modern styles, the melodic minor descends the same way as it ascends. An easy way to think of the ascending melodic minor is as a major scale with a flattened third degree.

T	S	T	T	T	T	S	T	T	S	T	T	S	T

A	B	C	D	E	F♯	G♯	A	G	F	E	D	C	B	A
1	2	♭3	4	5	6	7	1	♭7	♭6	5	4	♭3	2	1

THE HARMONIC MINOR SCALE

The raised 7th in the harmonic minor is not indicated in the key signature, instead it is shown as an accidental each time it occurs. In the key of A minor, all the notes are naturals except for the raised 7th degree, which is a **G♯**. The following example demonstrates two octaves of the A harmonic minor scale with each hand. The fingering is the same as that of the A natural minor scale.

79.   A Harmonic Minor

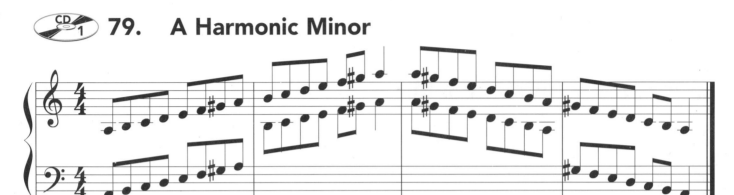

HARMONIC MINOR SCALE TONE CHORDS

Because there are three different minor scales, it is possible to come up with different sets of chords for a minor key by building chords on the notes of each different minor scale. Each variation to the notes of the scale alters the type of chords built on the scale. The letter names of the chords remain the same, but the chord type may change. E.g. shown below are scale tone chords derived from the **A harmonic minor scale**. Notice that chord III is now **augmented** (**C+**) instead of major, and also that chord V is **major** (**E**) instead of minor and chord VII is **diminished** (**G♯dim**) instead of major. These changes are all brought about by the raising of the 7th degree of the scale from **G** to **G♯**. The new chords are shown below in root position.

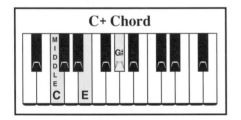
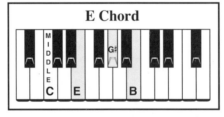
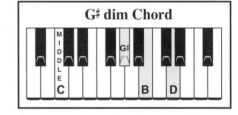

80.

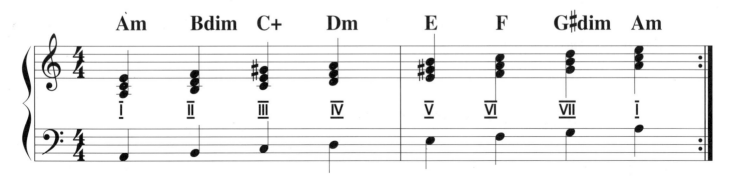

81.

Here is a piece derived from the A Harmonic minor scale and its scale tone triads.

82.

Like all chords, The scale tone chords derived from the harmonic minor scale can be arranged into inversions. Here are the inversions of the **E major** chord.

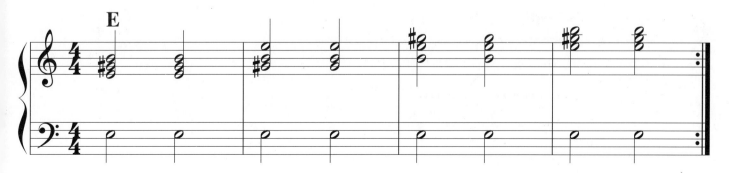

THE MELODIC MINOR SCALE

The ascending melodic minor scale contains raised **6th and 7th** degrees, neither of which appear in the key signature. In the key of A minor, these notes are **F♯** and **G♯**. Both notes are notated as accidentals. The following example demonstrates two octaves of the A melodic minor scale with each hand. Remember that the 7th and 6th degrees fall by a semitone when the scale descends

83.

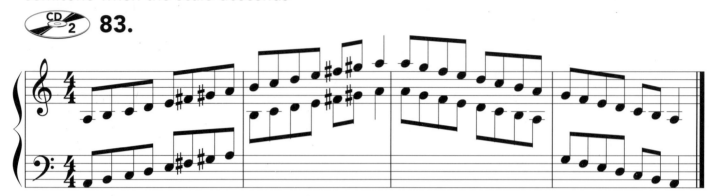

MELODIC MINOR SCALE TONE CHORDS

The scale tone chords derived from the **A melodic minor scale** are shown below. Because of the sharpened 6th degree, there will be more changes to the types of chords derived from this scale. Chord $\overline{\text{II}}$ is now **minor (Bm)** instead of major, chord $\overline{\text{IV}}$ is **major (D)** instead of minor and chord $\overline{\text{VI}}$ is **diminished (F♯dim)** instead of major. These changes are all brought about by the raising of the 6th degree of the scale from **F** to **F♯**.

84.

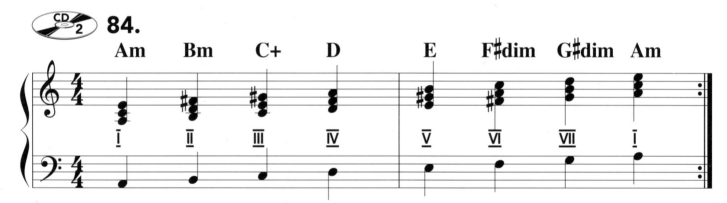

THE SIX EIGHT TIME SIGNATURE

6 8 This is the **six eight** time signature.
There are six eighth notes in one bar of $\frac{6}{8}$ time.
The six eighth notes are divided into two groups of three.

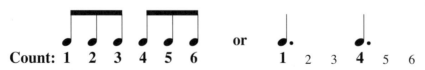

When playing $\frac{6}{8}$ time there are **two** beats within each bar, with each beat being a **dotted quarter note**. Note that this is different from $\frac{4}{4}$ and $\frac{3}{4}$ time, where each beat is a quarter note. **Accent** (play louder) the 1 and 4 count to help establish the two beats per bar.

85. House of the Rising Sun

When playing music in minor keys, it is common to use chords from all three types of minor scales. A good example of this is the song **House of the Rising Sun**. Look through the chords and see which ones come from each type of minor scale.

THE TWO FOUR TIME SIGNATURE

2/4 This is the **two four** time signature. It tells you there are **two** beats in each bar. In 2/4 time the note and rest values must add up to the equivalent of two quarter notes per bar.

 **86. First Loss**

R. Schumann

To end this section, here is a beautiful piece by **Robert Schumann** which is written in 2/4 time. It is in the key of **E minor** and contains chords from all three minor scale types. This piece contains a variety of musical terms and expressions. Take your time with it and learn the notes first without worrying about the tempo and dynamic markings. Practice any difficult parts one hand at a time and then play both hands together very slowly, bar by bar. Once you are confident you can play through the whole piece without mistakes, work on it concentrating purely on the expressive aspect, observing all the markings and exaggerating them at first until you have control of them.

RUBATO

When you play solo pieces, you don't have to keep such strict time as when you are playing with others. Sometimes you may wish to increase or decrease the tempo at certain points for dramatic effect. This is called **rubato**. Feel free to experiment with the time as you play, but make sure you are doing it for musical expression rather than because of technical inadequacies (e.g. slowing down for the difficult parts and speeding up for the easy parts - this is **not** a musical reason for using rubato!)

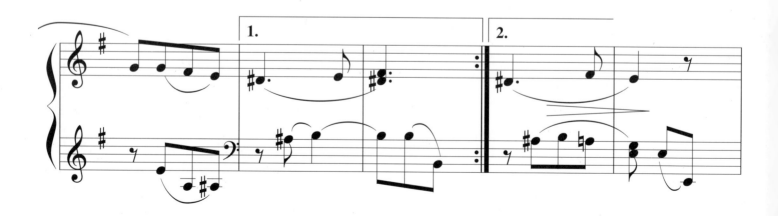

FOR FURTHER STUDY

Both this piece and the **Chorale** on page 84 come from Schumann's **Album for the Young** which is highly recommended. Even if you don't intend to play Classical music as your main style, you will get tremendous benefit from learning more of these pieces. You should also check out **JS Bach's Two Part Inventions**, and **Bela Bartok's Mikrokosmos**. These works will improve your technique, broaden your harmonic knowledge, and (in Bach's own words) "give you a strong foretaste of composition". If you do intend to pursue Classical music further, it is recommended that you do so with a teacher to guide you in regard to both technique and repertoire. In most countries there are systems of progressively graded exams for studying Classical music. Many people don't wish to sit exams, but the grades are an excellent guide to suitable pieces and technical studies for players of all levels.

SECTION 3

Blues, Rock and Boogie, Playing in all Keys

LESSON TWENTY SIX

THE MINOR PENTATONIC SCALE

So far all of the keyboard parts you have learnt have been based on chords and arpeggios. This is important because chords form the harmonic foundation of music. However, there are many parts based on scales instead of chords. A particularly useful scale is the **minor pentatonic** scale which is shown below in the key of A minor. This scale is used for many bass lines as well as being commonly used for soloing and improvisation. Whereas the major and natural minor scales contain seven different notes, pentatonic scales contain only **five**. The minor pentatonic scale can be thought of as a natural minor scale with the second and sixth degrees left out. The notes of the A minor pentatonic scale are **A C D E** and **G**.

1.0   **CD 2 Starts Here**

RIFFS

The following example shows how the A minor pentatonic scale can be used over a chord progression in the key of A minor. The repeated pattern of notes is called a **riff**. Riffs are common in many styles of music.

1.1   **(CD2)**

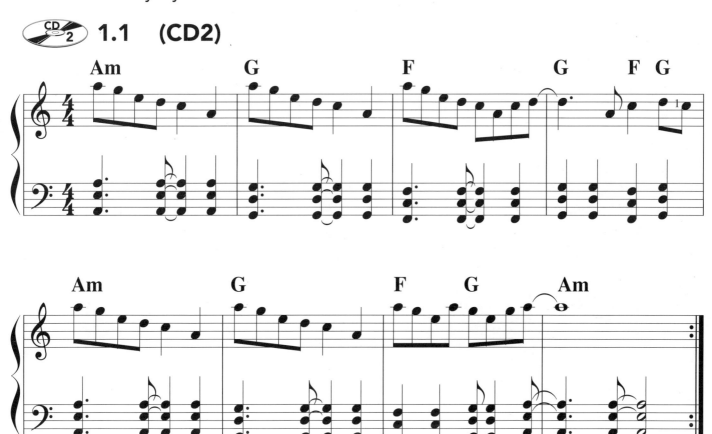

 **2.0**

Here is another example of a **riff** created from the minor pentatonic scale. This time the right hand plays a line which answers the left hand riff and then plays the riff along with the left hand.

Here are some more keyboard parts created from the minor pentatonic scale.

 **2.1**

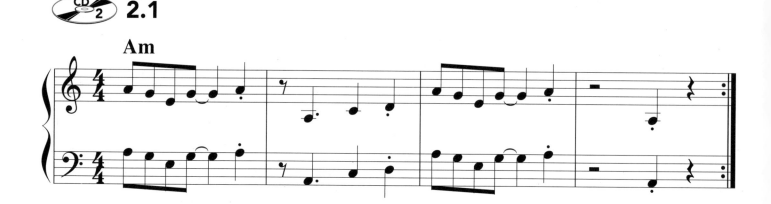

 **2.2**

This example contains a pattern where three notes of the A minor pentatonic scale are played by each hand in contrary motion. Try experimenting with other similar patterns. Notice that both parts are written in the treble staff for this example.

The following left hand pattern is great for improvising over. Practice the left hand by itself, then try playing some chords or pentatonic scale lines over it with the right hand as shown below

MINOR PENTATONIC SCALE IN E

Like all scales, the minor pentatonic scale can be transposed to any key. here is the **E** minor pentatonic scale.

 **4.0**

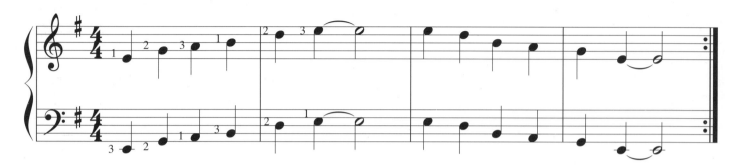

 **4.1**

Now try this example which is created entirely from the E minor pentatonic scale.

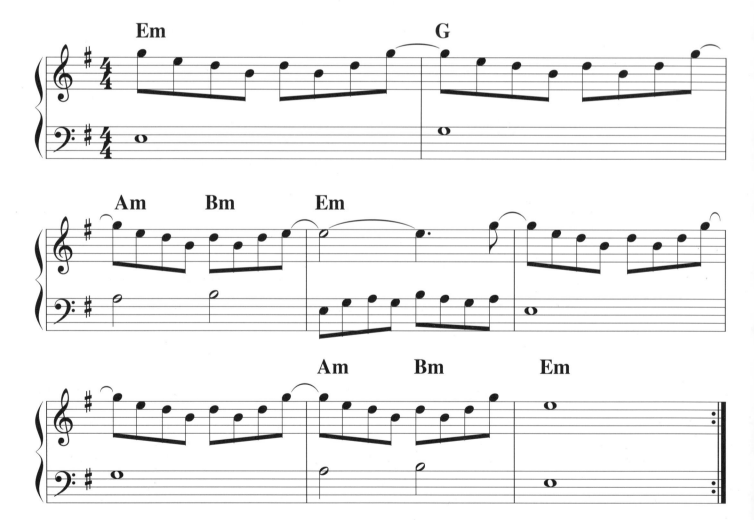

5.

Here is a 12 bar Blues which uses the E minor pentatonic scale to create lines over the left hand pattern from the previous lesson. Practice each hand separately if necessary.

LESSON TWENTY SEVEN

ALTERNATING OCTAVES

Another useful technique in Rock keyboard playing is the use of alternating octaves with the left hand. Written below is the **E natural minor** scale played in alternating octaves by the **5th** and **1st** fingers of the left hand.

 **6.0**

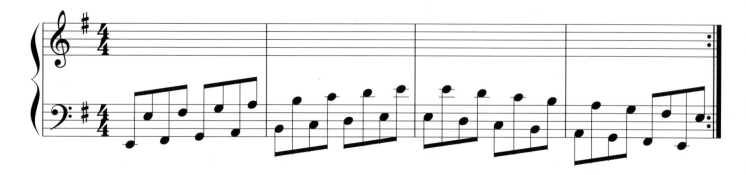

 **6.1**

Here is a keyboard part using alternating octaves. It will probably sound familiar to you.

 **6.2**

This example shows the same part transposed to the key of **A minor**.

7.

Using octaves on repeated notes is a great way to create a driving rhythm. The following 12 bar Blues shows chords played over an alternating octave left hand part. Take it slowly at first and practice each hand separately if necessary.

 **8.**

Here is another solo which uses an alternating octave left hand part. Co-ordinating the two hands may be difficult at first, so practice each hand separately if necessary. Once you can play it, try using the ideas and techniques to improvise with the right hand. You could also transpose the whole thing to A minor. The more you transpose and improvise with everything you learn, the more confident you will be in your keyboard knowledge and your ability to play with other musicians. Your eventual aim should be to be able to play any song or short piece you know in **any key**, and improvise on it. All good musicians can do this.

LESSON TWENTY EIGHT

MORE ABOUT 12 BAR BLUES

As you learnt in lesson 18, **12 Bar Blues** is a pattern of chords which repeats every 12 bars and may be played in any key. You have already learnt several examples of 12 bar Blues. There are hundreds of well known songs based on this chord progression, i.e., they contain basically the same chords in the same order. 12 bar Blues is commonly used in Blues, Jazz and Rock. Some popular songs which use the 12 bar Blues form are:

Original Batman TV Theme
Rock Around the Clock - Bill Haley
Johnny B Goode - Chuck Berry
Blue Suede Shoes - Elvis Presley
In the Mood - Glenn Miller
Surfin' USA - The Beach Boys

Rock in Peace - ACDC
Ice Cream Man - Van Halen
Killing Floor - Jimi Hendrix
Give Me One Reason - Tracy Chapman
Why Didn't You Call Me? - Macy Gray
Oh Pretty Woman - Gary Moore

 9.

Here is a 12 bar Blues in the key of **C**. The pattern of chords will probably sound familiar to you. The left hand part is a **walking bass** line. This technique is common in Blues and Jazz.

LEARNING THE BLUES FORM

As mentioned previously, the 12 bar Blues form can be applied to any key. The easiest way to do this is to memorize the chord pattern in roman numerals as shown below. Although there are many variations, the simplest form of the 12 bar Blues uses only chords Ī, ĪV and V̄.

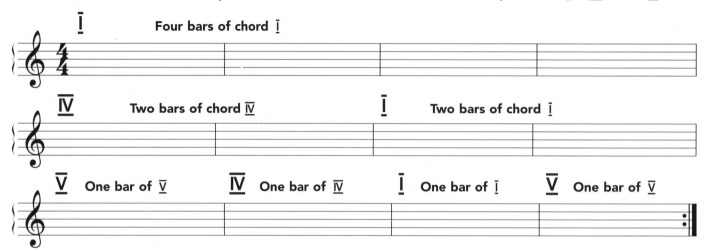

10.   12 Bar Blues in G

Here is a 12 bar Blues in the key of **G**. The chords are played with the right hand, while the left hand plays a common Blues and Boogie accompaniment pattern.

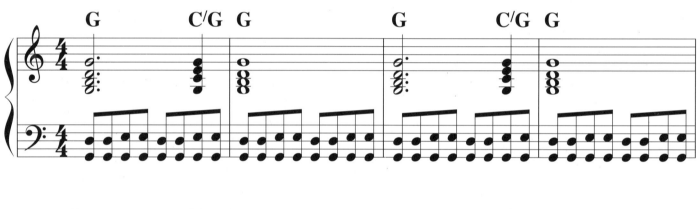

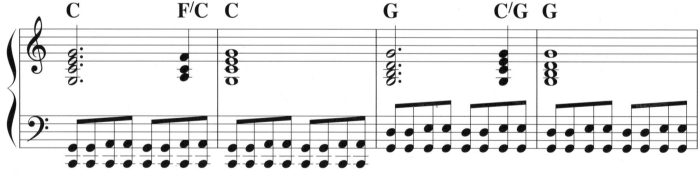

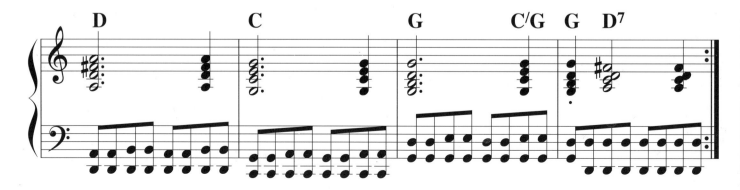

BLUE NOTES

flattened third ♭3   **flattened fifth** ♭5   **flattened seventh** ♭7
Blue notes   ♭3 which is **E♭**
in the key of C. listen to how effective it sounds when alternated with the natural 3rd degree (**E**).

CD2 **11.0**

CD2 **11.1**

This example uses the **flattened fifth (G♭)** and the **flattened seventh (B♭)** along with the flattened 3rd (**E♭**). Notice how effective blue notes sound when combined with harmony notes in bars 3 and 4. Once you can play this example, try improvising with chord tones and blue notes over an alternating octaves accompaniment. You should also do this with the left hand pattern from example 10 (CD2) first using one chord and then the 12 bar Blues form.

THE BLUES SCALE

One of the most practical ways of remembering the blue notes is to use the **Blues Scale**. It contains all three of the blue notes: ♭3, ♭5 and ♭7. The Blues scale can be played starting on **any** note. It is shown here in the key of **C**.

 **12.0**   **C Blues Scale**

It is worth comparing the notes of the Blues scale with those of the major scale. Here are the notes of both scales in the key of C.

C MAJOR SCALE

C	D	E	F	G	A	B	C
1	2	3	4	5	6	7	8

C BLUES SCALE

C	E♭	F	G♭	G	B♭	C
1	♭3	4	♭5	5	♭7	8

Notice that the Blues scale contains both the flat 5 and the natural 5. It does not contain the degrees 2 or 6. Altogether the Blues scale contains **six** different notes, whereas the major scale contains seven different notes. The major scale used by itself does not sound very bluesy. However, Blues melodies often contain notes from both of these scales. Listen to the following example to hear the difference between them.

 **12.1**

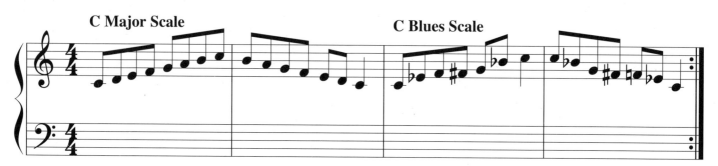

The following solo will help you become more comfortable with the Blues scale. The scale is played ascending and descending over the three bass notes **C**, **F** and **G** which are Ī , ĪV and V̄ in the key of C. Notice how changing the bass note alters the sound. Notice also the use of octaves in the left hand part. Practice each hand by itself at first if necessary.

13.

LESSON TWENTY NINE

THE TRIPLET

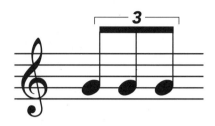

An eighth note triplet is a group of three evenly spaced notes played within one beat. Eighth note triplets are indicated by three eighth notes with the number **3** written either above or below the group. Sometimes the triplet has a bracket or a curved line around the number 3. The notes are played with a third of a beat each.

 14.0

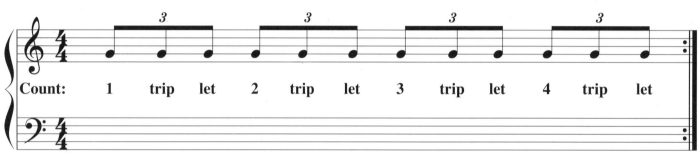

 14.1

Here are some 7th chords played with a triplet rhythm.

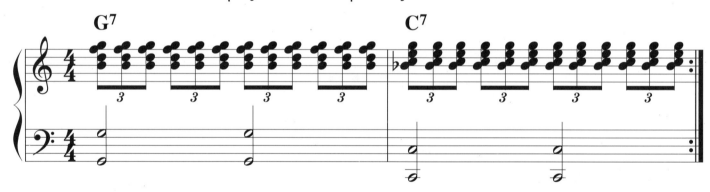

 14.2

Triplets sound great when combined with the notes of the Blues scale. Listen to the following example and then make up some of your own triplet based riffs from the Blues scale.

SWING RHYTHMS

Since the early 20th century there have been many new styles of music which use a rhythmic feeling called **swing**. These styles include Blues, Jazz, Gospel, Soul, Rock and Funk. A **swing rhythm** is created by tying together the first two notes of a triplet. There are several different ways of writing swing rhythms. To understand them it is worth using one musical example written in various ways. The example below has the first and second notes of the triplet group tied together. Play this example and listen to the feeling created by the rhythm.

15.0

Instead of tying the first two notes of the triplet group, a quarter note can be used. The quarter note grouped with an eighth note by a triplet bracket shows clearly that the first note is worth two thirds of the beat, while the second note is worth only one third. Play the following example and notice that it sounds the same as the previous one.

15.1

A third way to write the same rhythm is to notate the whole thing in eighth notes and to write ♫ = ♩♪ at the start of the music. Jazz players usually write swing rhythms in this manner, as it is easier to read. Play example 15.2 and notice that once again it sounds the same.

15.2

THE SHUFFLE

By playing a constant stream of swinging eighth notes, an effect known as the **Shuffle** can be created. A good way to start coordinating both hands when playing a shuffle is to play the **shuffle rhythm** with the **left hand** and **triplets** with the **right hand**. Both hands coincide on the **first** and **third** part of each triplet.

17.

Here is another shuffle, this time written differently. Notice the use of the 7th of each chord in the left hand part. If you have trouble with this one, practice each hand separately at first.

LESSON THIRTY

IMPROVISATION

To become a good Blues player, it is important to develop the ability to improvise. A good way to do this is to use the right hand to improvise short lines with the Blues scale while playing a shuffle with the left hand. First, practice the scale itself over one chord, then use the whole 12 bar progression.

 **18.0**

Here is a Blues scale idea played over a shuffle left hand part for a C chord.

 **18.1**

This time, the initial triplet figure is repeated to create a longer variation.

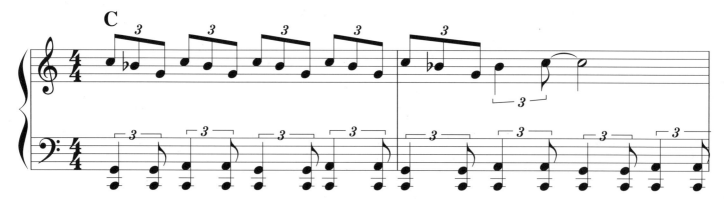

CD 2 **19.**

Here is a 12 bar Blues solo which makes use of these techniques. By this time you know enough to start improvising your own Blues solos. You could use any of the ideas presented so far as a starting point. The main thing is to experiment and have fun with the music, remembering that the more you do it, the better you get. It also helps to have some kind of a theme in your playing and to develop it through repetition and variation.

LESSON THIRTY ONE

SEVENTH CHORDS

Chord Symbol

7

Chord Formula

1	3	5	♭7

After triads, the next most common chord type is the **seventh chord**, (sometimes called the dominant seventh chord). Seventh chords consist of **four notes** taken from the major scale of the same letter name. These notes are the first (**1**), third (**3**), fifth (**5**) and **flattened seventh** (♭**7**) notes of the major scale, so the **chord formula** for the seventh chord is:

$$1 \quad 3 \quad 5 \quad ♭7$$

A flattened seventh (♭**7**) is created by lowering the seventh note of the major scale by one semitone. This is the same ♭**7** note that is found in the Blues scale. Notice that the seventh chord is simply a major chord with a flattened seventh note added.

Chord Symbol

G7

THE G SEVENTH CHORD (G7)

Notes in Chord

G	B	D	F
1	3	5	♭7

The **G7** chord can be constructed from the G major scale. Using the seventh chord formula on the G major scale gives the notes **G**, **B**, **D** and **F**. When the seventh note of the G major scale (**F♯**) is flattened, it becomes an **F** natural.

Note Name	G	A	B	C	D	E	F♯	G
Note Number	1	2	3	4	5	6	7	8
Seventh Chord Formula	1		3		5		♭7	
G Seventh Chord	G		B		D		F	

Play the notes of the **G7** chord with the **first**, **second**, **fourth** and **fifth** fingers of your right hand, individually and then together as shown below.

 **20.0**

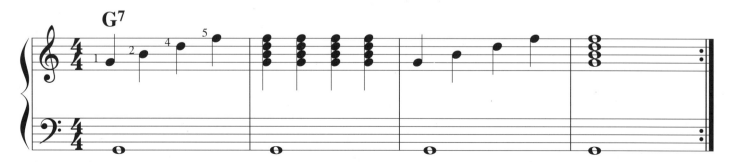

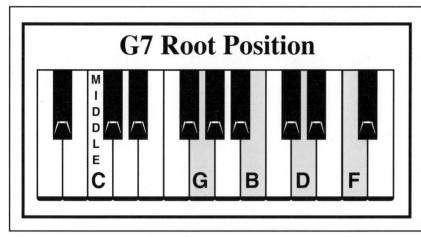

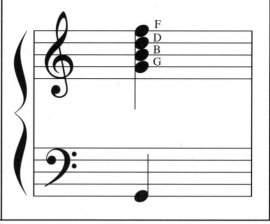

G7 CHORD INVERSIONS

Because the **G7** chord contains **four notes**, there are **three inversions** plus the root position. The following three diagrams illustrate the first inversion (3 5 ♭7 1), the second inversion (5 ♭7 1 3), and the third inversion (♭7 1 3 5) of the G7 chord.

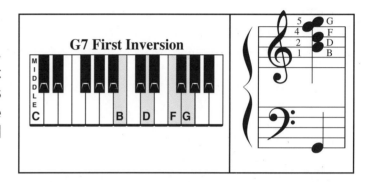

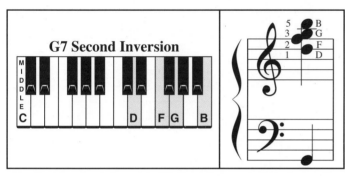

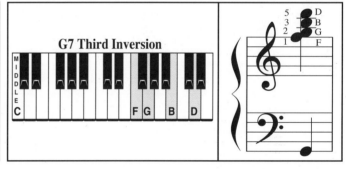

The example below uses all the inversions of the G7 chord. Use the correct fingerings as shown in the diagrams.

 **20.1**

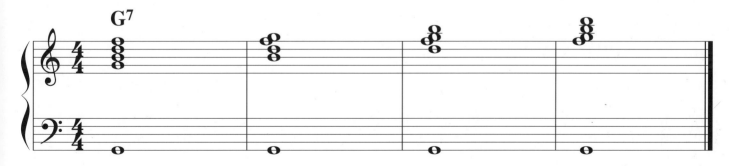

Seventh chords are particularly common in Blues, Boogie and Rock 'n' Roll piano playing. The example below demonstrates a 1st inversion **G7** chord played over the left hand pattern you have been using, this time played as straight eighth notes.

THE C7 CHORD

Like G7, the **C7** chord contains the degrees 1, 3, 5 ♭7. Its notes are C, E, G and B♭. Here are the four basic positions of the C7 chord.

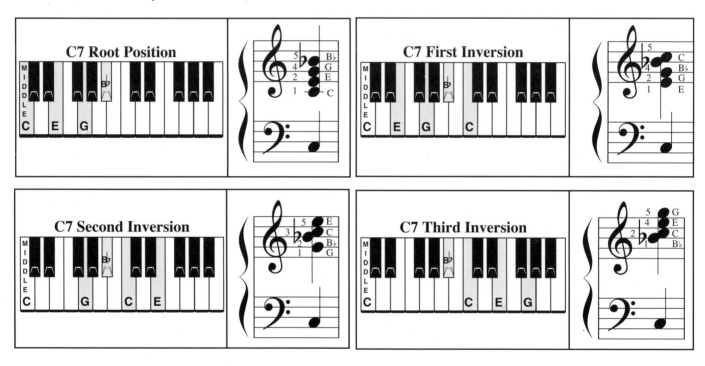

THE F7 CHORD

Here are the four basic positions for the **F7** chord. Its notes are F, A, C and E♭.

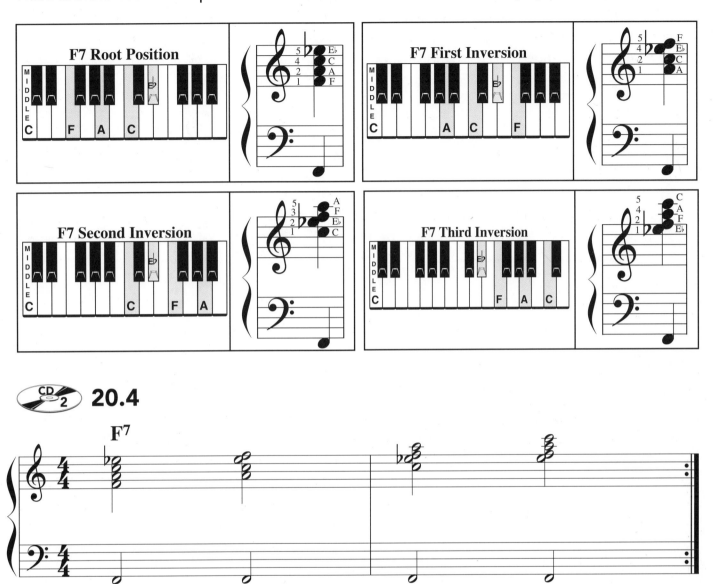

20.4

OMITTING NOTES FROM CHORDS

Because there are four notes in a 7th chord, they are often more difficult to play than major chords. When using 7th chords it is common to leave out one of the notes. The most commonly omitted note is the 5th, although sometimes the 3rd or the root can be omitted. Usually the left hand will be playing the root note anyway. As long as the ♭7 degree is in the chord you still get the effect of a 7th chord. Here are some examples of partial 7th chords.

20.5

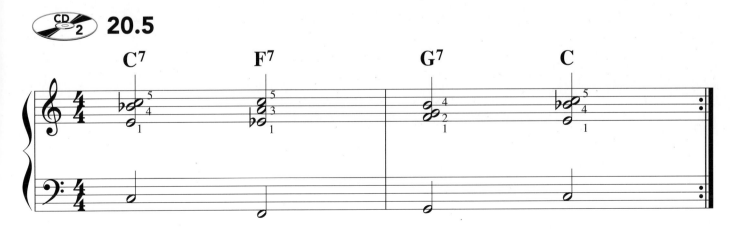

21.

Listen to how good these chords sound when applied to a 12 bar Blues progression. Learn this example and then experiment with different rhythms using the same chords, as well as different inversions using the same rhythms. Feel free to leave out any note other than the ♭**7** when using any of the inversions.

BUILDING 7TH CHORDS ON OTHER NOTES

Like major and minor chords, 7th chords can be built on any of the 12 notes used in music. By memorizing the formula for a 7th chord (**1 3 5 ♭7**) and choosing a root note to apply the formula to, you can create **A7**, **E7**, **F♯7**, **B♭7** or any other 7th chord. An easy way to learn 7th chords is to notice that a 7th chord is simply a major chord with an extra note added a **minor 3rd** interval above the 5th of the chord (3 semitones). All 7th chords have four possible inversions, which gives you a variety of positions and fingerings for playing them. Shown below are the four inversions of a **D7** chord.

THE D7 CHORD

The notes of a D7 chord are D (1), F♯ (3), A (5) and C (♭7). Here are the four basic positions for a D7 chord.

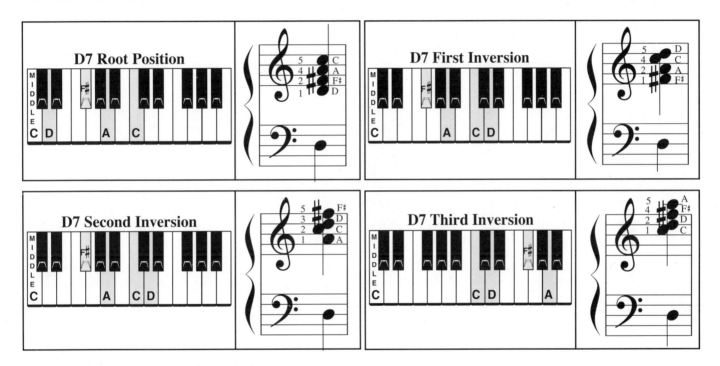

22.

LESSON THIRTY TWO

GRACE NOTES

The use of **grace notes** is an important expressive technique in all styles of keyboard playing. Grace notes have no real time of their own. Rather, they are heard as an expression added to the note they are leading to. A grace note is indicated by a very small note with a stroke through its stem. This note is played immediately before the following note, which is held for its full value.

 **23.0**

There are two basic ways of playing grace notes. In Blues it is very common to play a grace note on a black key and then slide off onto a white key with the same finger. This technique is not used in classical piano playing, but is important in Blues playing.

*Play D♯ note
with 2nd finger.*

*Slide finger off
to sound E note.*

 **23.1**

The second technique does come from classical piano music. It involves playing a grace note on a white note and following it with either a black note or another white note. Each note is played with a different finger.

*Play D note
with 2nd finger.*

*Play E♭ note
with 3rd finger.*

Here are some of the ways grace notes are commonly used in Blues and Boogie.

142

Here is a 12 bar Blues solo which makes use of grace notes. The eighth notes in this example are played straight (i.e. not swung) Notice the new left hand pattern here. This pattern is common in Rock 'n' Roll and Boogie piano playing.

25.

LESSON THIRTY THREE

LEFT HAND PATTERNS

In Blues and Boogie piano playing, there are many different left hand patterns which can be used. Here are some common ones with a simple right hand part played over them. Learn each one from memory and then apply it to the 12 bar Blues progression. When you are comfortable with each new left hand part, try it with some of the right hand parts from earlier lessons, and then try improvising over it. It is also important to repeat this process in many different keys. Playing in all keys is dealt with in lesson 35.

CD 2 26.0

CD 2 26.1

Most of these left hand patterns work equally well swung or played straight - experiment.

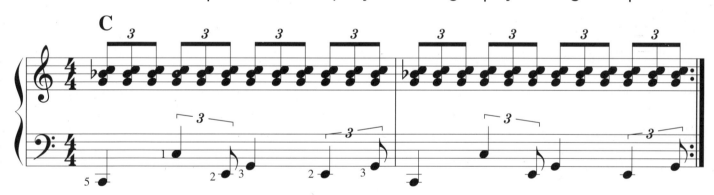

CD 2 26.2

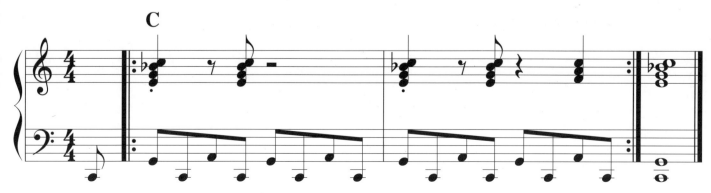

26.3

26.4

26.5

Here is a two bar pattern which works well both straight and swung. These are just a few of the left hand patterns used in Blues and Boogie piano playing. It is important to listen to albums featuring keyboard players and learn to copy what they are doing. You should also constantly experiment and make up your own parts. The more you do this, the easier it gets.

SIXTEENTH NOTE TRIPLETS.

Triplets can be created on any note value. A **sixteenth note triplet** is three sixteenth notes played evenly across the space usually taken by two sixteenth notes. This means that the triplet grouping lasts for the same duration as an eighth note. It is common for two sixteenth note triplets to occur together as a group of six notes across one quarter note beat. To count a sixteenth note triplet, say **Did - dle - a**, for two sixteenth note triplets across a beat, say **Did - dle - a - Did - dle - a**.

 **27.**

Say: Did - dle - a Did - dle - a Daa, Did - dle - a Did - dle - a Daa.

Here are some typical ways sixteenth note triplets are used in Blues. Practice them slowly with a metronome until you can play them perfectly and then use the ideas to improvise.

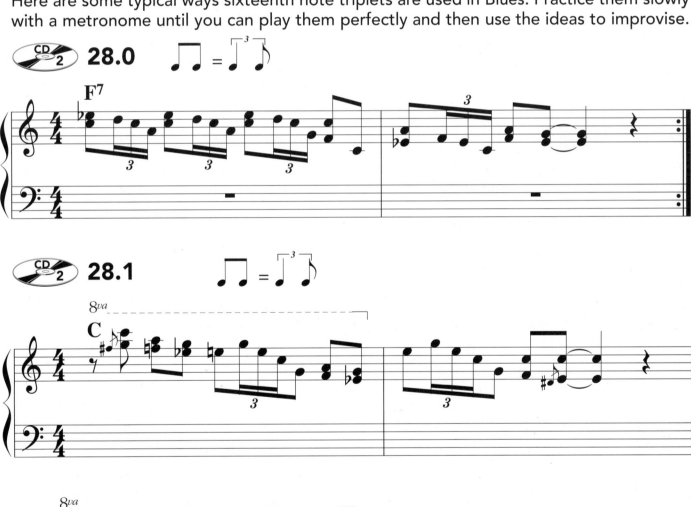

 **29 New Orleans Blues**

This New Orleans style Blues solo is a real challenge. It contains a new note value - the 32nd note, which is half the value of a 16th note. To hear this style at its best, listen to players like **Professor Longhair**, **James Booker** and **Dr John**.

THE GLISSANDO

Another important expressive technique is the **glissando** (**gliss** for short). This is simply a slide either to or away from a note. A gliss is usually done with the nail of the thumb, supported by the whole hand. On an organ, or electric keyboard, the side of the hand can often be used. Use the left hand when ascending and the right when descending. Get a teacher or experienced player to demonstrate it for you, as it can be painful if done incorrectly. The gliss is indicated by a wavy diagonal line leading either to a note or away from a note. Listen to the following example on the CD to hear the effect it produces.

THE TRILL AND THE TREMOLO

Two other techniques commonly used in keyboard playing are the **trill** and the **tremolo**. Both consist of a rapid alternation between two notes. For smaller intervals such as 2nds and 3rds, the term **trill** is used, and the effect is achieved purely by finger action. With larger intervals such as 6ths and Octaves, the term **tremolo** is used, and it is achieved with a wrist motion. As with the glissando, it is best to have someone demonstrate these techniques for you. Both take some time to gain control of, so be patient and practice them for a short time each day. The trill and tremolo are indicated by two diagonal lines through the stems of the notes involved. The following example uses these techniques along with the glissando.

Note: In Classical music, there are several variations on the trill (called **ornaments**). There are specific ways of notating each one. They are best learnt with the aid of a teacher.

 **32.** **Blues For Otis**

Here is a Blues piano solo which features glissandi, trills and tremolo. Notice the new left hand pattern here. Practice each hand separately until you are comfortable with both parts.

LESSON THIRTY FOUR

16TH NOTE STUDIES

Here are some exercises to help you become more familiar with 16th note groupings. Count out loud as you play each one and tap your foot to help you keep time. It would also be useful to practice them with a metronome or drum machine. If you are serious about music you should be using a metronome for everything you practice. A musician with good control of rhythm and timing is always popular with other musicians.

 **33.**

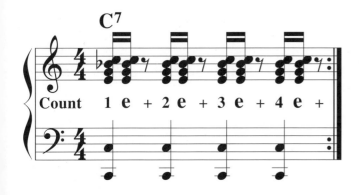

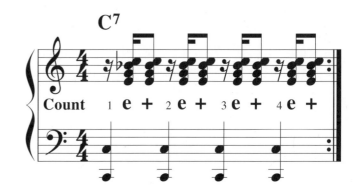

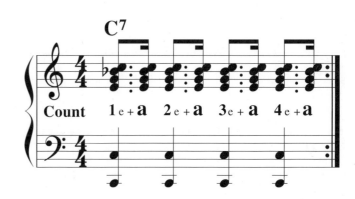

Once you are comfortable with these basic 16th note groupings, it is easy to create great sounding keyboard parts using simple patterns. Here are some examples.

 **34.0**

 **34.1**

Notice the **F** note in the chord under the **C7** symbol in this example. This is called a **suspension**, which means substituting the 4th degree for the 3rd. Suspended chords are discussed in lesson 39.

The following examples demonstrate parts which feature much interplay between both hands. Practice them slowly at first with a metronome and gradually increase the tempo until you can play them along with the CD.

 **35.0**

 **35.1**

This one is a variation on the previous example.

 **35.2**

Here is a slightly more complex line based around a C minor arpeggio.

36.0

In this one the right hand plays full chords but both hands are still working together.

36.1

This one takes the same type of idea even further.

 **37.**

This Gospel style 12 bar Blues is based on an underlying 16th note rhythm. Take it slowly to begin with, and practice each hand separately with a metronome if you need to.

LESSON THIRTY FIVE

PLAYING IN ALL KEYS

Once you know the pattern of tones and semitones used to create the C major scale, you can build a major scale on **any** of the twelve notes used in music. It is important to memorize this pattern, which is shown below.

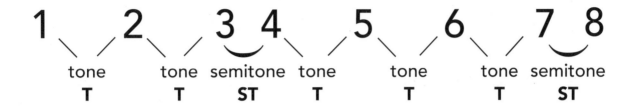

The **semitones** are always found between the **3rd and 4th**, and **7th and 8th** degrees of the scale. All the other notes are a tone apart.

By simply following the pattern of tones and semitones, it is possible to construct a major scale starting on any note. The scale will be named by the note it starts on. The following example demonstrates four more major scales.

CD 2 **38.**

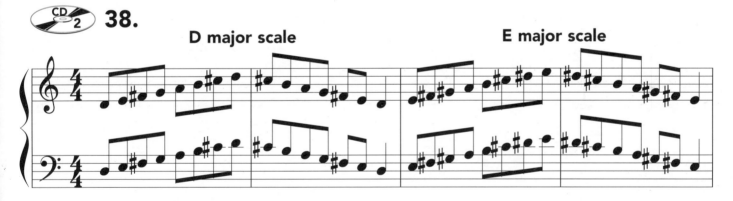

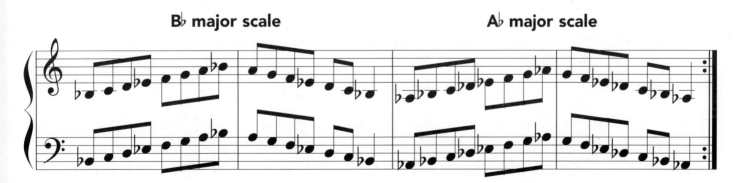

Now that you know how major scales are constructed, try writing major scales built on the notes **A**, **B**, **F♯**, **E♭**, **D♭** and **G♭**. Some will contain sharps, while others will contain flats. Remember that the scale is named from its starting note and all you have to do is follow the pattern of tones and semitones.

MORE ON KEYS AND KEY SIGNATURES

The **key** describes the note around which a piece of music is built. Remember that when a piece of music consists of notes from a particular scale, it is said to be written in the **key** which has the same notes as that scale. The key signature is written at the start of each line of music, just after the clef.

The number of sharps or flats in any key signature depends on the number of sharps or flats in the corresponding major scale. The major scales and key signatures for the keys of **F** and **G** are shown below. Without sharps and flats, these scales would not contain the correct pattern of tones and semitones which gives the major scale its distinctive sound.

G Major Scale

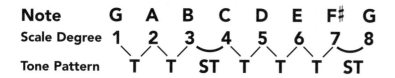

Key Signature of G Major

The **G major** scale contains one sharp, F♯, therefore the key signature for the key of **G major** contains one sharp, F♯.

F Major Scale

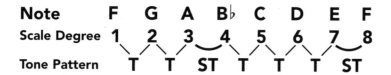

Key Signature of F Major

The **F major** scale contains one flat, B♭, therefore the key signature for the key of **F major** contains one flat, B♭.

Some scales contain sharps while others contain flats because there has to be a separate letter name for each note in the scale. E.g. the G major scale contains F♯ instead of G♭ even though these two notes are identical in sound. If G♭ was used, the scale would contain two notes with the letter name G and no note with the letter name F. In the key of F major, the note B♭ is chosen instead of A♯ for the same reason. If A♯ was used, the scale would contain two notes with the letter name A and no note with the letter name B.

The charts on the following page contain the **key signatures** of all the major scales used in music, along with the number of sharps or flats contained in each key. Because there are 12 notes used in music, this means there are 12 possible starting notes for major scales (including sharps and flats). Note that some of the keys will have sharps or flats in their name, e.g. F♯ major, B♭ major, E♭ major, etc. Keys which contain sharps are called sharp keys and keys which contain flats are called flat keys.

The key signatures for all the major scales that contain sharps are:

The sharp key signatures are summarised in the table below.

*The new sharp **key** is a fifth interval * higher*

Key	Number of Sharps	Sharp Notes
G	1	F♯
D	2	F♯, C♯
A	3	F♯, C♯, G♯
E	4	F♯, C♯, G♯, D♯
B	5	F♯, C♯, G♯, D♯, A♯,
F♯	6	F♯, C♯, G♯, D♯, A♯, E♯

*The new sharp **note** is a fifth interval higher*

Written below are the key signatures for all the major scales that contain flats.

The flat key signatures are summarised in the table below.

*The new flat **key** is a fourth interval higher*

Key	Number of Flats	Flat Notes
F	1	B♭
B♭	2	B♭, E♭
E♭	3	B♭, E♭, A♭
A♭	4	B♭, E♭, A♭, D♭
D♭	5	B♭, E♭, A♭, D♭, G♭,
G♭	6	B♭, E♭, A♭, D♭, G♭, C♭

*The new flat **note** is a fourth interval higher*

The following example demonstrates one octave of the major scale ascending and descending in every key. Learning scales may not seem as interesting as playing tunes, but a little effort at this stage will pay off very well later on. Memorize the fingering for each scale and then try playing it with your eyes closed while imagining how the notation for the scale would look. Once you have learnt all the scales, you will be able to play melodies confidently in any key and be able to improvise in any key much more easily.

39. Major Scales in all Keys

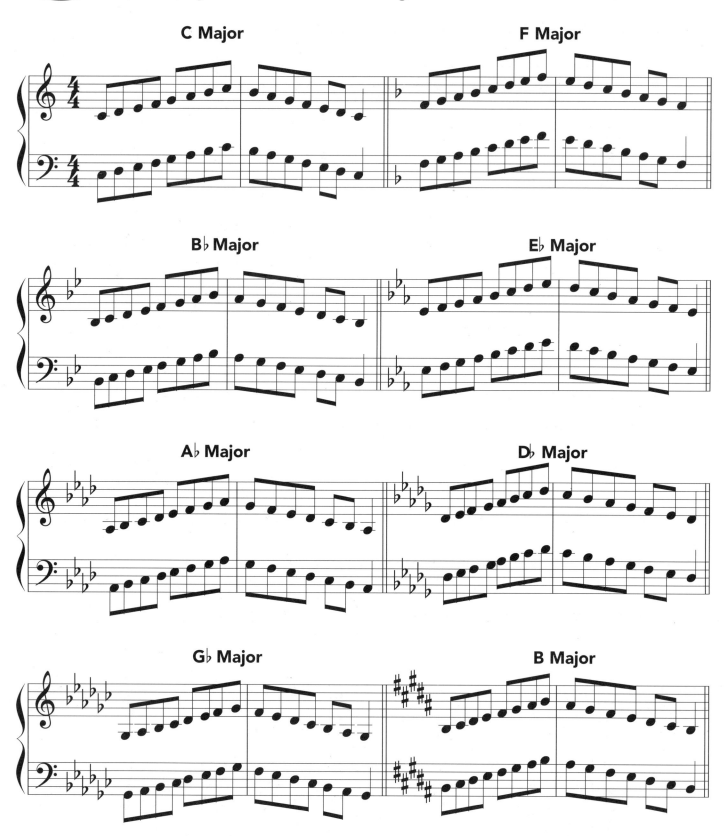

The scales shown in the above example are only one octave. However, it is important to practice scales over the entire length of the keyboard and also to break them up into sequences. It is recommended that you obtain a book of scales, arpeggios and exercises such as **Hanon** (any teacher will know this book) and practice them in all keys if you wish to become a great keyboard player, as they will give you the technique and knowledge of keys that you need to be fluent when improvising. It also helps to memorize the names of the notes in each scale. The chart below lists the notes in all major scales.

MAJOR SCALES CHART

	T	T	S	T	T	T	S
C MAJOR	C	D	E	F	G	A	B	C
G MAJOR	G	A	B	C	D	E	F#	G
D MAJOR	D	E	F#	G	A	B	C#	D
A MAJOR	A	B	C#	D	E	F#	G#	A
E MAJOR	E	F#	G#	A	B	C#	D#	E
B MAJOR	B	C#	D#	E	F#	G#	A#	B
F# MAJOR	F#	G#	A#	B	C#	D#	E#	F#
F MAJOR	F	G	A	Bb	C	D	E	F
Bb MAJOR	Bb	C	D	Eb	F	G	A	Bb
Eb MAJOR	Eb	F	G	Ab	Bb	C	D	Eb
Ab MAJOR	Ab	Bb	C	Db	Eb	F	G	Ab
Db MAJOR	Db	Eb	F	Gb	Ab	Bb	C	Db
Gb MAJOR	Gb	Ab	Bb	Cb	Db	Eb	F	Gb
Scale Degrees	I	II	III	IV	V	VI	VII	VIII

MORE ABOUT RELATIVE KEYS

In lesson 24 you learned that the **A natural minor** scale and the **C major** scale contain the same notes; the only difference is that they start on a different note. This is why these two scales are referred to as "relatives"; **A minor** is the **relative minor** of **C major** and vice versa.

Major Scale: C Major

Relative Minor Scale: A Natural Minor

The harmonic and melodic minor scale variations are also relatives of the same major scale, e.g. the **A harmonic** and **A melodic minor** scales are all relatives of **C major**.
For every major scale (and ever major chord) there is a relative minor scale which is based upon the **6th note** of the major scale. This is outlined in the table below.

MAJOR KEY (I)	C	Db	D	Eb	E	F	F#	Gb	G	Ab	A	Bb	B
RELATIVE MINOR KEY (VI)	Am	Bbm	Bm	Cm	C#m	Dm	D#m	Ebm	Em	Fm	F#m	Gm	G#m

Both the major and the relative minor share the same key signature, as illustrated below.

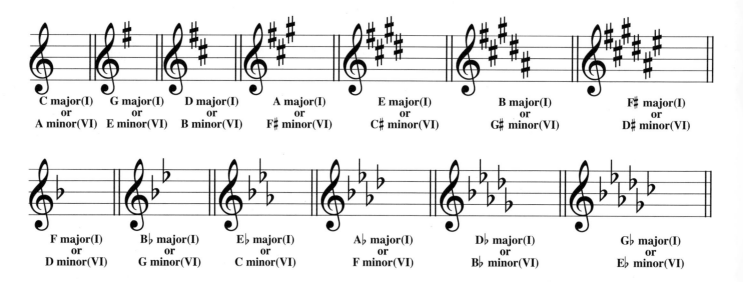

To determine whether a song is in a major key or the relative minor key, look at the **last** note or chord of the song. Songs often finish on the root note or the root chord which indicates the key. E.g., if the key signature contained one sharp, and the last chord of the song was **Em**, the key would probably be **E minor**, not **G major**. Minor key signatures are always based on the natural minor scale. The sharpened 6th and 7th degrees from the harmonic and melodic minor scales are **not** indicated in the key signature. This usually means there are accidentals (temporary sharps, flats or naturals) in melodies created from these scales.

CD 2 40.

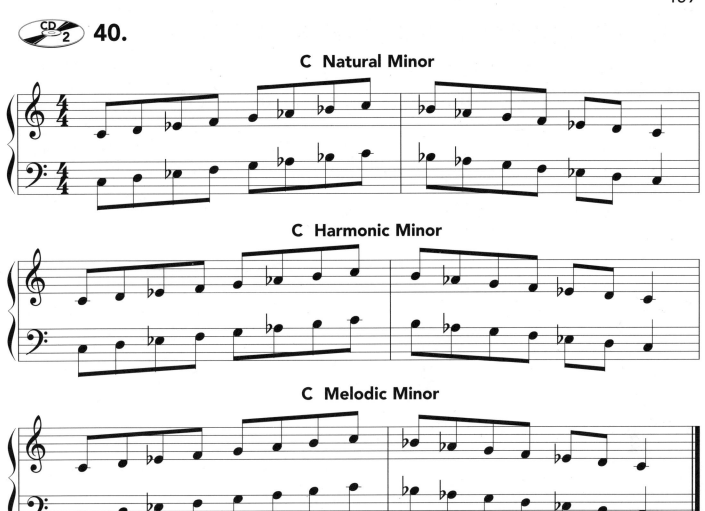

MINOR SCALES CHART

The following chart shows the notes of the traditional melodic minor scale in all twelve keys. Remember that the **descending melodic minor is the same as the natural minor**. To work out the notes for the **harmonic minor**, simply **flatten the 6th** degree of the ascending melodic minor. Once again, it is recommended that you purchase a copy of **Hanon** and familiarize yourself with all the minor scales and their fingerings.

	T	S	T	T	T	T	S	T	T	S	T	T	S	T
A MELODIC MINOR*	A	B	C	D	E	F#	G#	A	G♮	F♮	E	D	C	B	A
E MELODIC MINOR*	E	F#	G	A	B	C#	D#	E	D♮	C♮	B	A	G	F#	E
B MELODIC MINOR*	B	C#	D	E	F#	G#	A#	B	A♮	G♮	F#	E	D	C#	B
F# MELODIC MINOR*	F#	G#	A	B	C#	D#	E#	F#	E♮	D♮	C#	B	A	G#	F#
C# MELODIC MINOR*	C#	D#	E	F#	G#	A#	B#	C#	B♮	A♮	G#	F#	E	D#	C#
G# MELODIC MINOR	G#	A#	B	C#	D#	E#	G	G#	F#	E♮	D#	C#	B	A#	G#
D# MELODIC MINOR	D#	E#	F#	G#	A#	B#	D	D#	C#	B♮	A#	G#	F#	E#	D#
D MELODIC MINOR*	D	E	F	G	A	B♮	C#	D	C♮	B♭	A	G	F	E	D
G MELODIC MINOR*	G	A	B♭	C	D	E♮	F#	G	F	E♭	D	C	B♭	A	G
C MELODIC MINOR	C	D	E♭	F	G	A♮	B♮	C	B♭	A♭	G	F	E♭	D	C
F MELODIC MINOR	F	G	A♭	B♭	C	D♮	E♮	F	E♭	D♭	C	B♭	A♭	G	F
B♭ MELODIC MINOR	B♭	C	D♭	E♭	F	G♮	A♮	B	A♭	G♭	F	E♭	D♭	C	B♭
E♭ MELODIC MINOR	E♭	F	G♭	A♭	B♭	C♮	D♮	E♭	D♭	C♭	B♭	A♭	G♭	F♭	E♭
Scale Degrees	İ	İİ	İİİ	İV	V	Vİ	Vİİ	Vİİİ	Vİİ	Vİ	V	İV	İİİ	İİ	İ

LESSON THIRTY SIX

THE KEY CYCLE

There are many reasons why you need to be able to play equally well in every key. Bands often have to play in keys that suit their singer. That could be **F#** or **D♭** for example. **E** and **A** are common keys for guitar, while horn players like flat keys such as **F**, **B♭** and **E♭**. As well as this, certain styles (particularly Jazz and Fusion) contain many key changes in themselves. For these reasons, you need to learn how keys relate to each other so you can move quickly between them.

One way to do this is to use the **key cycle** (also called the **cycle of 5ths** or **cycle of 4ths**). It contains the names of all the keys.

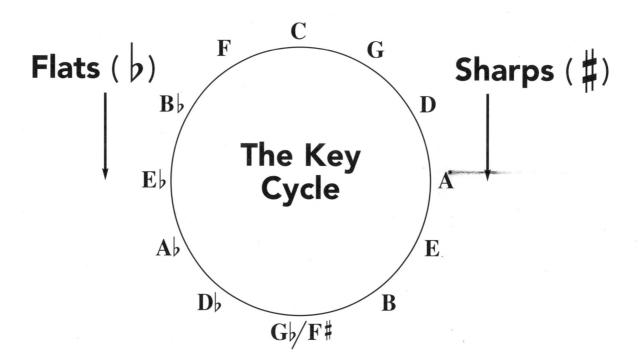

To help memorize the key cycle, think of it like a clock. Just as there are 12 points on a clock, so there are 12 keys. **C** is at the top and contains no sharps or flats. Moving around clockwise you will find the next key is **G**, which contains one sharp (**F#**). The next key is **D**, which contains two sharps (**F#** and **C#**). Progressing further through the sharp keys, each key contains an extra sharp, with the new sharp being the 7th note of the new key, and the others being any which were contained in the previous key. Therefore the key of A would automatically contain **F#** and **C#** which were in the key of D, plus **G#** which is the 7th note of the A major scale. When you get to **F#** (at 6 o'clock), the new sharp is called **E#** which is enharmonically the same as **F**. Remember that **enharmonic** means two different ways of writing the same note - ie, **F#** = **G♭**. Thus the key of **F#** contains six sharps, while the key of **G♭** contains six flats – all of which are exactly the same notes.

If you start at **C** again at the top of the cycle and go anti-clockwise you will progress through the flat keys. The key of **F** contains one flat (**B♭**), which then becomes the name of the next key around the cycle. In flat keys, the new flat is always the 4th degree of the new key. Continuing around the cycle, the key of **B♭** contains two flats (**B♭** and **E♭**) and so on. **Practice playing all the notes around the cycle both clockwise and anticlockwise**. Once you can do this, play chords starting on each note of the cycle, as shown on the following page.

PLAYING CHORDS IN ALL KEYS

To be comfortable playing in all keys, it is important to be able to play any type of chord built on any note of the chromatic scale. A good way to practice chords is to choose a chord type (e.g. major triads) and play them around the key cycle either clockwise, or anticlockwise as shown in the following example. Say the name of each chord out loud as you play it. The chords are all shown here in root position, but it is essential to practice all inversions of each chord in the same manner, i.e. play first inversion triads around the cycle, then second inversion triads.

41.

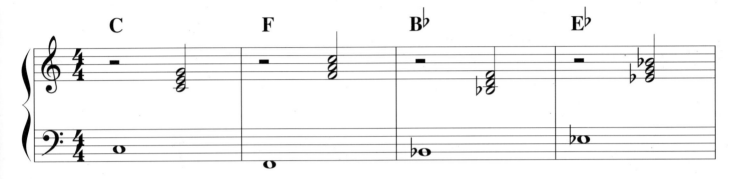

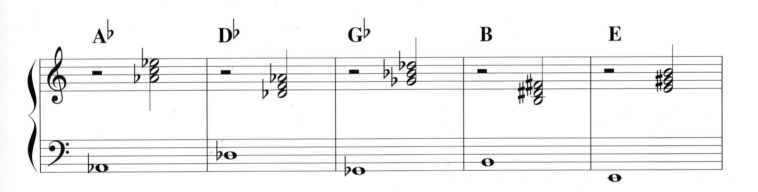

162

Once you can play each inversion of a chord in any key, the next step is to play a chord type around the key cycle using inversions which are close together on the keyboard. This means using different inversions within the same chord sequence. There are three ways of doing this exercise, each one starting on a different inversion of the same chord. E.g. if you play major triads around the cycle starting with a **root position C chord**, the closest **F chord** is a **second inversion** and the closest **G chord** is a **first inversion**. The following example demonstrates major triads played around the key cycle anticlockwise in this manner.

 **42.0**

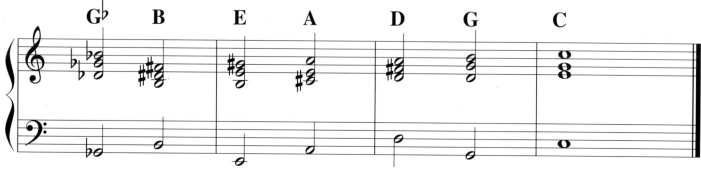

 **42.1**

This time the chords are played with the **left hand**, starting with a first inversion C chord. It is important to be able to play chords equally well with both hands, so make sure you practice all chord exercises this way as well.

43.

This example demonstrates first inversion minor triads played clockwise around the key cycle. Remember to practice root position and second inversion minor triads as well. Although only major and minor triads are shown in this lesson, it is important to practice **diminished** and **augmented** chords in this manner also.

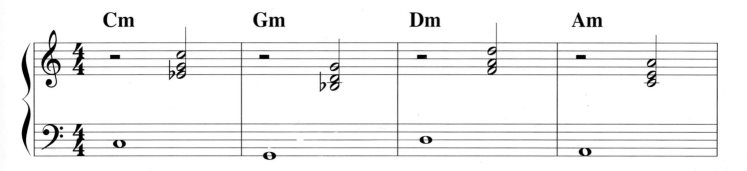

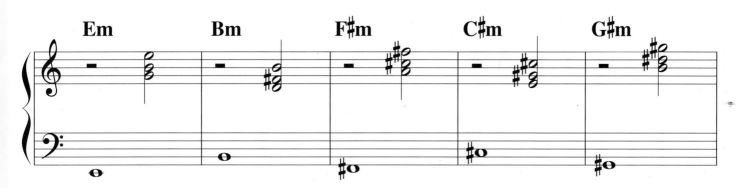

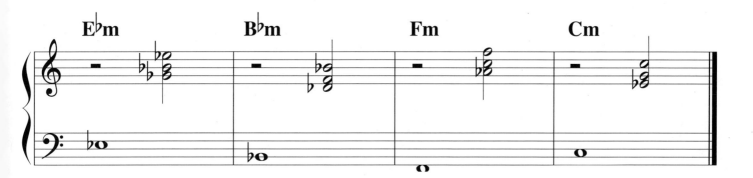

As well as playing chords around the key cycle, it is also useful to practice each inversion chromatically up or down, in major 2nds up or down, minor 3rds up or down and major 3rds up or down. When you select these intervals, the chords will divide into two, three or four groups. E.g. if you play major triads down in major seconds, one group will consist of **C**, **B♭**, **A♭**, **G♭**, **E** and **D**, while the other group will consist of **D♭**, **B**, **A**, **G**, **F** and **E♭**.

LESSON THIRTY SEVEN

SCALE TONE CHORDS IN ALL KEYS

Once you are familiar with playing different types of chords around the key cycle, the next step is to put them to practical use. The best way to start this is to learn the scale tone chords of each major and minor key. This is obviously a long term project, but if you work steadily at it, you will be amazed at the results within a few months. Shown below is the triad pattern for major keys. Learn it from memory and then apply it to all major scales as shown in the table at the bottom of the page.

MAJOR KEY TRIAD PATTERN

I	Major	(C Major Chord)
II	Minor	(D Minor Chord)
III	Minor	(E Minor Chord)
IV	Major	(F Major Chord)
V	Major	(G Major Chord)
VI	Minor	(A Minor Chord)
VII	Diminished	(B Diminished Chord)

SCALE TONE TRIADS IN ALL KEYS

Scale Degree	I	II	III	IV	V	VI	VII	VIII (I)
Chord Constructed:	major	minor	minor	major	major	minor	dim	major
C Scale	C	Dm	Em	F	G	Am	B°	C
G Scale	G	Am	Bm	C	D	Em	F#°	G
D Scale	D	Em	F#m	G	A	Bm	C#°	D
A Scale	A	Bm	C#m	D	E	F#m	G#°	A
E Scale	E	F#m	G#m	A	B	C#m	D#°	E
B Scale	B	C#m	D#m	E	F#	G#m	A#°	B
F# Scale	F#	G#m	A#m	B	C#	D#m	E#° (F°)	F#
F Scale	F	Gm	Am	B♭	C	Dm	E°	F
B♭ Scale	B♭	Cm	Dm	E♭	F	Gm	A°	B♭
E♭ Scale	E♭	Fm	Gm	A♭	B♭	Cm	D°	E♭
A♭ Scale	A♭	B♭m	Cm	D♭	E♭	Fm	G°	A♭
D♭ Scale	D♭	E♭m	Fm	G♭	A♭	B♭m	C°	D♭
G♭ Scale	G♭	A♭m(G#m)	B♭m	C♭ (B)	D♭	E♭m	F°	G♭

PRIMARY CHORDS

In any key there are some chords which are more commonly used than others. The three most common chords are $\underline{\mathrm{I}}$, $\underline{\mathrm{IV}}$ and $\underline{\mathrm{V}}$. These are the **primary chords**. With these three chords, it is possible to harmonize (accompany with chords) any melody in the key, because between them they contain every note of the scale, as shown below in the key of **C**.

C Major Scale   **C D E F G A B C**

Primary Triads

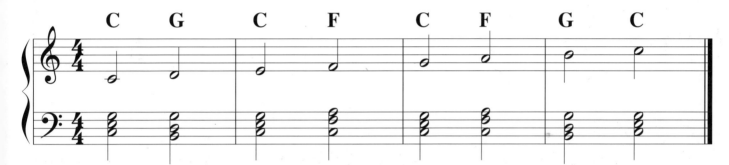

 **44.0**

The table below shows the primary chords in all twelve major keys.

PRIMARY TRIADS IN ALL MAJOR KEYS

KEY	$\underline{\mathrm{I}}$	$\underline{\mathrm{IV}}$	$\underline{\mathrm{V}}$	KEY	$\underline{\mathrm{I}}$	$\underline{\mathrm{IV}}$	$\underline{\mathrm{V}}$
C	C	F	G	F	F	B♭	C
G	G	C	D	B♭	B♭	E♭	F
D	D	G	A	E♭	E♭	A♭	B♭
A	A	D	E	A♭	A♭	D♭	E♭
E	E	A	B	D♭	D♭	G♭	A♭
B	B	E	F♯	G♭	G♭	C♭	D♭
F♯	F♯	B	C♯				

 **44.1**

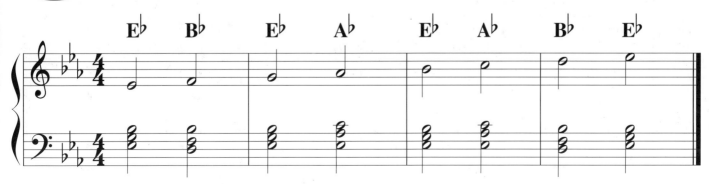

HARMONIZING MELODIES

To harmonize a melody, you simply play a chord which contains a note from that melody on the **first beat of each bar**. In $\frac{4}{4}$ time, you could also add another chord on the **third** beat of the bar. There is always more than one chord which could be used, but some sound better than others. The more songs you learn and analyze, the easier it becomes to find the right chords to play. If you analyze the primary chords in C major, you will notice that the notes **C** and **G** appear in two chords. This means that when harmonizing a melody in the **key of C**, you could try both chords wherever one of these notes appear on the first beat of a bar. The following example shows a melody in C major harmonized with chords $\bar{I}$, $\overline{IV}$ and $\bar{V}$.

45.0

45.1

Once you are happy with the basic chords, you can use them to create a more interesting accompaniment. Here the left hand plays a pattern using the **root** and **5th** of each chord.

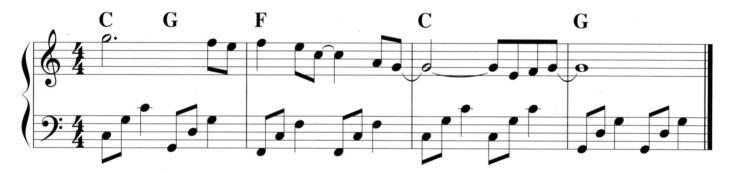

45.2

You could also add extra harmony notes using voice parts, as well as adding some responses to the melody, or bass runs. Experiment with different approaches to harmonizing other melodies you know. The more you do it, the easier it gets.

LESSON THIRTY EIGHT

DOMINANT 7THS AS CHORD $\overline{V}$

In styles other than Blues and Jazz, Dominant 7ths are most commonly built on the 5th degree of both major and minor scales. In this situation the chord is described as $\overline{V7}$. The example below demonstrates an **E7** chord (notes **E**, **G**♯, **B** and **D**) as chord $\overline{V7}$ in the key of **A minor**. All of the notes of the chord are contained in the **A harmonic minor** scale. It is simply an E major triad with a **D** note added a minor 3rd above the B. The chords used here are the three primary chords in the key of A minor.

 **46.**

To familiarize yourself with 7th chords in all keys, play all four inversions around the key cycle until you are comfortable with them. The example below uses inversions which are close together on the keyboard. This produces the smoothest sound and is also more practical than jumping around for the sake of keeping the same inversion for each chord.

 **47.**

7TH CHORD ARPEGGIOS

Like all chords, Dominant 7ths can be played as arpeggios. The following example demonstrates each inversion of an **A7** chord and then a 3 octave arpeggio covering all inversions of the chord.

48.

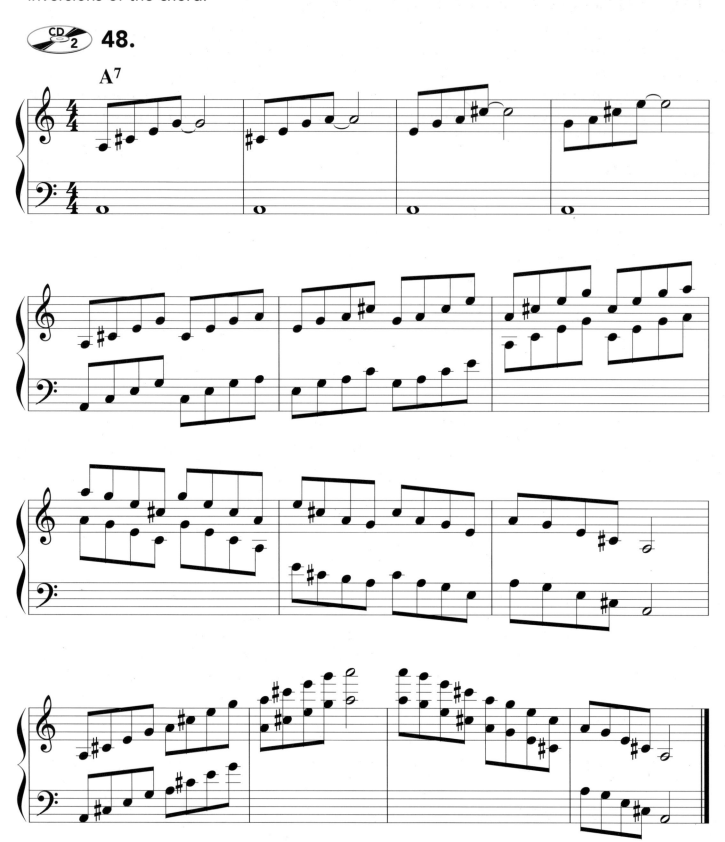

Once you are comfortable playing 7th chords around the cycle, try using them as chord $\overline{V}$ of a key when harmonizing melodies and creating parts. Here is an example played in the key of **C** and then transposed to **E♭**. Notice also the use of a **sus4** (suspended) chord in these examples. These chords are discussed in the following lesson.

LESSON THIRTY NINE

SUSPENDED CHORDS

By substituting the 4th degree of a scale for the 3rd of either a major or minor chord, a **suspended chord** (**sus** or **sus⁴**)can be created. Suspended chords work well in both major and minor keys. Listen to the example below to hear the effect of a suspended chord.

 **50.0**

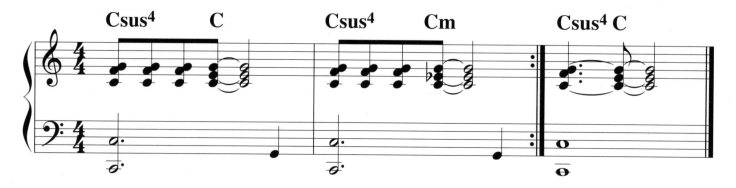

ADD 9 CHORDS

Another sound which is related to suspended chords is the addition of the ninth degree to either a major or minor triad. This creates an **add9** chord when applied to a major triad, or a **minor add9** chord when applied to a minor triad. The **ninth** degree of a scale is a duplication of the **second** degree an octave higher. However, when using the 9th degree, it may appear in any octave and may be played by either hand. Chords extending past the octave will be dealt with in more detail in the following lesson. Here is an example which demonstrates both major and minor **add9** chords.

 **50.1**

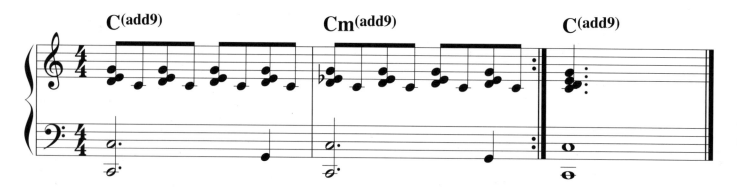

51.

Here is a piano part which uses both suspended and add9 chords. Bar 4 features an **A♭sus2** chord, in which the added 9th (2nd) replaces the 3rd of the chord.

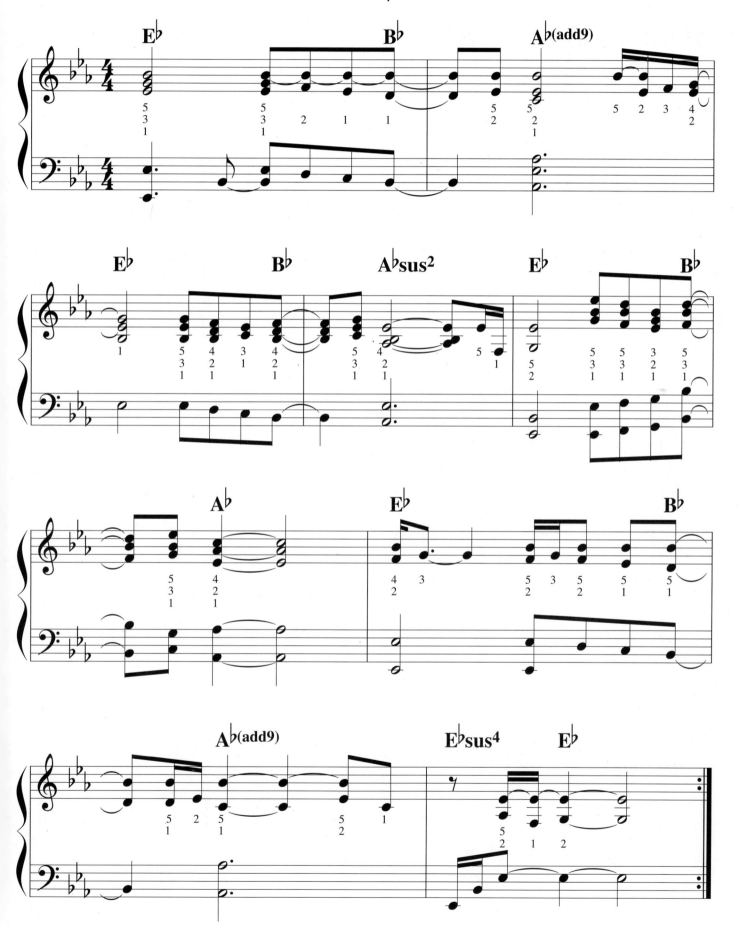

LESSON FORTY

SECONDARY CHORDS

Although most melodies can be harmonized using only chords Ī, IV̄ and V̄ , it is also common to use one or more of the remaining chords (IĪ, IIĪ, VĪ and VIĪ) to create a different feeling. These other chords are called **secondary chords**. As with primary chords, the secondary chord chosen for the harmony in any given bar should contain the melody note which occurs on the first or third beat of that bar (wherever the chord changes). Here is a simple melody in the key of C harmonized with chords Ī, IV̄ and V̄ .

52.0

In order to re-harmonize a melody, you need to know all the chords which contain each note. Shown below are all seven scale tone chords in the key of C. Notice that each note of the scale is contained in three different chords; e.g. the note **C** is the **root** of chord Ī (**C**), the **3rd** of VĪ (**Am**) and the **5th** of IV̄ (**F**).

G	A	B	C	D	E	F
E	F	G	A	B	C	D
C	D	E	F	G	A	B
Ī	IĪ	IIĪ	IV̄	V̄	VĪ	VIĪ

Here is the same melody harmonized with a mixture of primary and secondary chords. Notice how the different harmony changes the feeling of the melody as well.

52.1

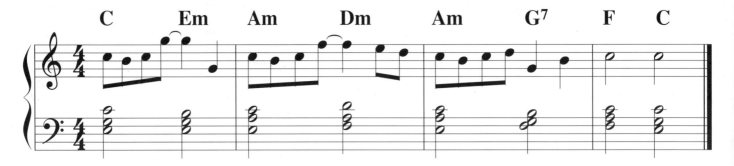

The table of scale tone chords from the previous page can be applied to any key. The easiest way to transpose any melody or chord is to think in degrees rather than note names. Here is a numbered version of the table which applies to all keys. In time, you should memorize this as it will make harmonizing any melody a lot quicker and easier.

5	6	7	1	2	3	4
3	4	5	6	7	1	2
1	2	3	4	5	6	7
I	II	III	IV	V	VI	VII

By using this table, it is easy to transpose both melody and chords to any other key. Here is example 52.0 transposed to the key of A♭ major. Learn it in this key and then transpose it to all the other keys. Make a habit of playing everything you know in all keys. As with everything else, the more you do it, the easier it gets.

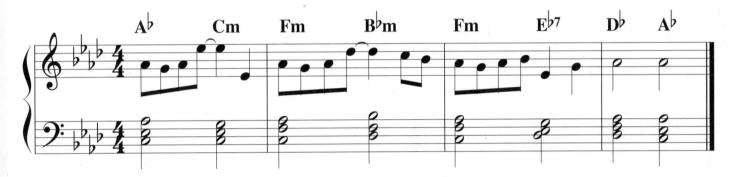

COMMON PROGRESSIONS

One of the best ways to become familiar with chords in all keys is to take a simple progression and transpose it to all of the keys. This may be slow at first, but the more you do it, the easier it gets. Here are some common progressions to learn and transpose. Remember to practice them in different ways, e.g with either hand, both hands together and as arpeggios.

I IV V I   I VI IV V   I V VI IV   I VI II V   I IV VII III VI II V

52.2

Once you have learned any basic progression, experiment with finding different ways of using it to create music. Here is another version of the same melody, this time accompanied by a bass line derived from the chords and connected with **passing notes** from the C major scale. There are always many different ways to play a chord progression.

SECONDARY DOMINANTS

In lesson 38 You learned that dominant 7ths most frequently occur as chord $\overline{V}7$ of a major or minor key. However, it is possible to substitute a dominant 7th chord for any scale tone chord (e.g. $\overline{II}7$, $\overline{III}7$, or $\overline{VI}7$. These are referred to as **secondary dominants**. The use of secondary dominants is useful for implying a series of $\overline{V}$ $\overline{I}$ progressions in different keys, while harmonizing a melody which stays within one key. Secondary dominants can be used in any style of music, and are particularly common in Jazz and Blues. Here is a progression demonstrating the use of secondary dominant chords.

 **53.**

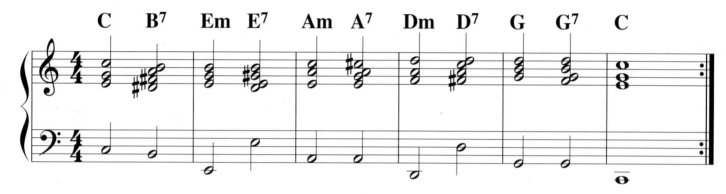

TWELVE EIGHT TIME ($\frac{12}{8}$)

Another useful time signature is **twelve eight time** ($\frac{12}{8}$). It tells you there are **twelve eighth note beats** in each bar. A bar of eighth notes in twelve eight time sounds the same as a bar of triplets in four four time. Although there are twelve individual beats which can be counted, twelve eight time is usually still counted in four (**1** 2 3 **2** 2 3 **3** 2 3 **4** 2 3). Notice the use of secondary dominant chords throughout this piece. Notice also the use of the **8vb** symbol which tells you to play the indicated notes **one octave lower** than written.

 **54.**

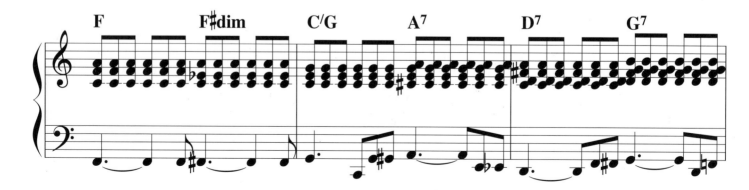

LESSON FORTY ONE

SEVENTH CHORD TYPES

By adding more notes on top of the basic triads, it is possible to create many other types of chords. After triads, the next most common chords are seventh chords. Various types of seventh chords are created by adding another note either a major or minor third above the basic triad. The formulas for the various types of seventh chords are shown below and on the following page. Like triads, once you have memorised each one, practice it in all inversions and transpose it to other keys.

Major Seventh
Chord Formula

Chord Symbol

CMaj7

1 3 5 7

Notes in Chord

C	E	G	B
1	3	5	7

Dominant Seventh
Chord Formula

Chord Symbol

C7

1 3 5 ♭7

Notes in Chord

C	E	G	B♭
1	3	5	♭7

Minor Seventh
Chord Formula

Chord Symbol

Cm7

1 ♭3 5 ♭7

Notes in Chord

C	E♭	G	B♭
1	♭3	5	♭7

Minor Seven Flat Five
Chord Formula

Chord Symbol

Cm7♭5

1 ♭3 ♭5 ♭7

Notes in Chord

C	E♭	G♭	B♭
1	♭3	♭5	♭7

The final type of seventh chord is the diminished seventh. This chord is unusual in that it contains a **double flattened 7th** degree (♭♭7). This note is actually the same as the 6th degree (A) but it is technically called **B♭♭7** because the interval has to be some kind of seventh rather than a sixth because the chord is a type of **seventh** chord.

Diminished Seventh
Chord Formula

Chord Symbol

C°7

1 ♭3 ♭5 ♭♭7

Notes in Chord

C	E♭	G♭	B♭♭
1	♭3	♭5	♭♭7

The following example demonstrates all five 7th chord types in root position. Notice how changing one new note each time creates a new chord. Learn the formula for each chord type from memory and then build them on all twelve notes of the chromatic scale.

 55.   Moving Between 7th Chord Types

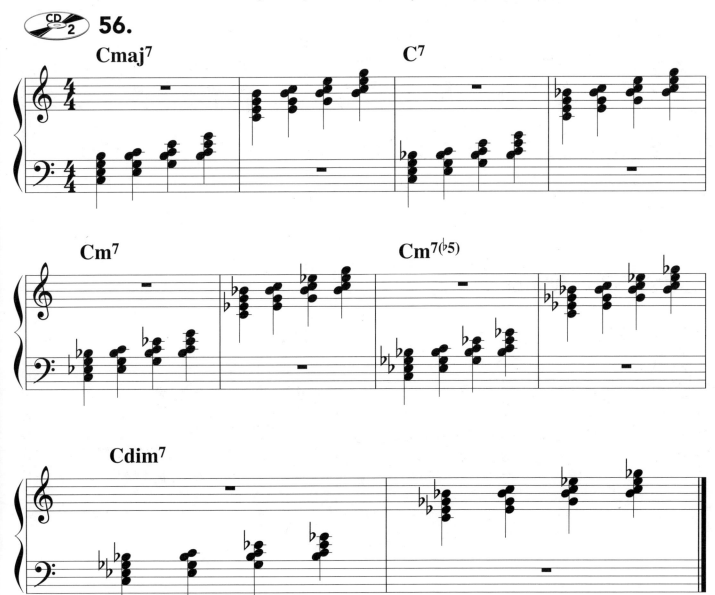

INVERSIONS OF 7TH CHORD TYPES

All 7th chord types can be played by either hand in **four** possible inversions, as demonstrated below. Once you can play this example, memorize the inversions for each type individually and transpose them to all keys. This is quite a task, but is essential if you wish to play Jazz. Do it for a few minutes each day and you will be surprised how quickly you learn them.

56.

The most commonly used types of 7th chord are the Dominant 7th, the Major 7th and the Minor 7th. However, it is important to know how to use all the various types of 7th chords. Here are some examples which demonstrate parts using each of the seventh chord types. The first one makes use of major 7ths.

57.0 Major 7

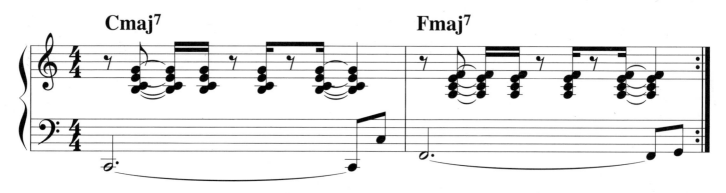

57.1 Dominant 7

57.2 Minor 7

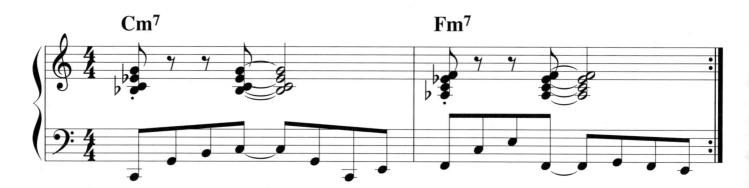

57.3 Minor 7 Flat 5

57.4 Diminished 7

58. Rhythm Changes

Here's one using all five types of 7th chords. This is a common Jazz progression known as **Rhythm Changes**. It originally came from the **George Gershwin** song **I Got Rhythm**, and has been used as the basis for many other songs over the years. Once you can play it, transpose it to all the other keys.

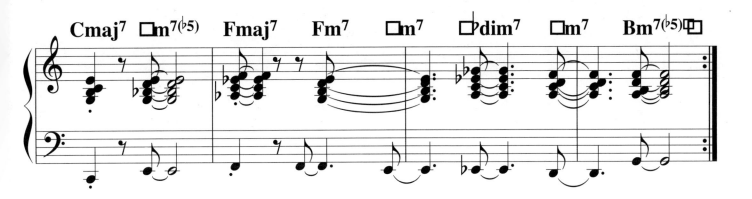

SCALE TONE SEVENTH CHORDS

By applying the formulas for seventh chords to the C major scale, the following series of chords is created. These are called **scale tone seventh chords**.

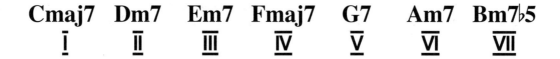

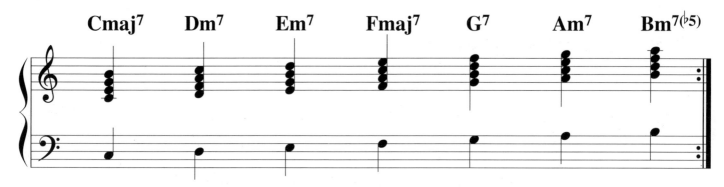

Here are some examples which use these chords. The first one is a II V I progression, which is the most common progression in Jazz and is also found in many other styles.

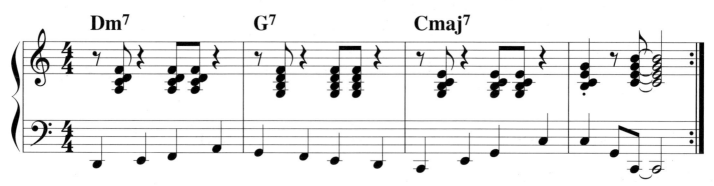

This one is based on another common progression: I VI II V. Learn it and then transpose it to all the other keys. Do the same with the previous example as well.

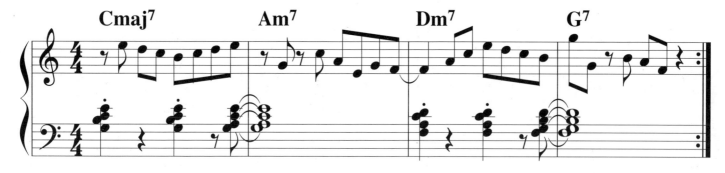

61. 7th Arpeggios Exercise

Here are the scale tone 7ths in the key of C played as arpeggios. Once again, it is important to know these in all keys. Make a habit of transposing everything you learn to all twelve keys.

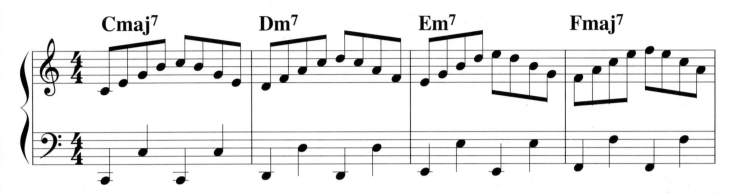

62.0

Once you know the notes of an arpeggio, the next step is to improvise with it. This example demonstrates an improvised line created from a **Dm7** arpeggio.

62.1

The next step is to improvise with chord tones over chord progressions. This one is based on a II̲ V̲ I̲ progression.

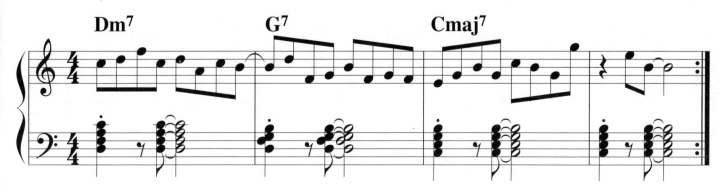

GUIDE TONES

As you know, it is possible to omit non essential notes from chords. Any type of 7th chord can be implied simply by playing the **3rd** and **7th**. These are the **guide tones** - the 3rd tells you whether the triad is major or minor, while the 7th tells you what type of 7th is used above the triad. In the case of a **m7♭5** chord and a **dim7** chord, the 5th can also be a guide tone, but in major, minor and dominant 7ths, the 5th can be omitted. Using guide tones makes it possible to create smooth chord progressions. The 3rd of one chord often progresses to the 7th of the next chord and vice versa as shown below.

63.0

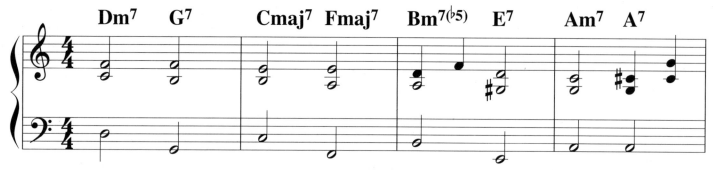

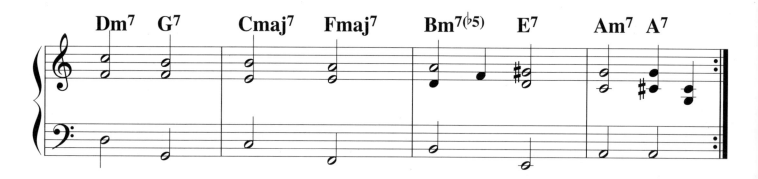

63.1

Some interesting voicings can also be created by **doubling** one of the guide tones.

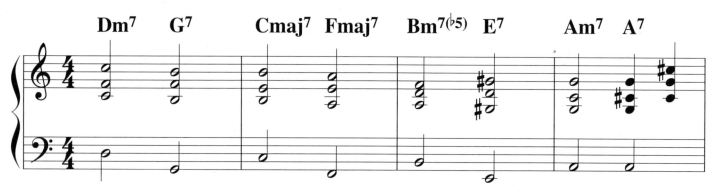

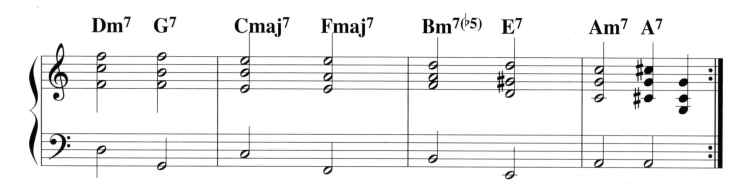

CHORD SUBSTITUTION

If you analyze the notes of scale tone 7th chords, you will notice that they are all based on the C major scale tone triads and each one has another 3rd interval added above it. If the left hand is playing the root of each chord, it is possible to leave the root note out of the right hand voicing. A common method of playing 7th chords it to use **only triads** with the **right hand** and play the root note with the left hand. If you choose the triad **two notes ahead** in the scale of the key you are working in, you can imply a 7th chord. This is called **chord substitution**. E.g. for a **CMaj7** chord, play a **C bass note** with the left hand and an **Em triad** instead of a CMaj7 with the right hand. The combined notes are **C, E, G, B**, which is a **CMaj7** chord. This could also be described as **Em/C** . A comparison is shown below.

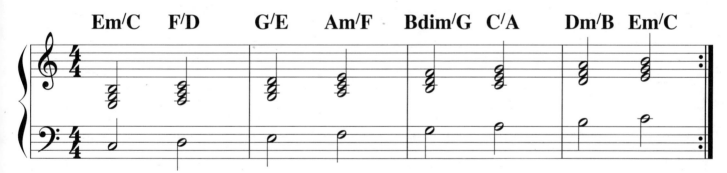

 **64.0**

This example shows how substituting the scale tone triad two ahead can be applied to the C major scale. The same principle applies to all keys.

 **64.1**

Most slash chords add up to another chord type (e.g. some kind of 7th chord). Sometimes it makes more sense to describe the chord as a slash chord, (e.g. when a pedal tone is being used) and other times it makes more sense to describe the chord as what the notes add up to. The following example demonstrates both a slash chord (**F/C**) and a minor 7th chord created by substituting an **Eb** triad for a **Cm7** in the right hand part.

SCALE TONE 7TH PATTERN

Like triads, the pattern of scale tone 7th chord types remains the same for every key. The pattern is summarized below. The minor 7 flat 5 chord is also sometimes called a half diminished chord (ø7).

I	II	III	IV	V	VI	VII	VIII
major7	m7	m7	maj7	7	m7	m7♭5 or (ø7)	maj7

The following chart shows scale tone 7th chords in all keys. If you intend to play Jazz, or any kind of Fusion music, it is essential to memorize all these chords. Work through each key and then take a simple progression and play it in every key. Then try a longer progression, then a song containing the various 7th chord types. After a while it will be able to do it without even thinking.

SCALE TONE 7THS IN ALL KEYS

I	II	III	IV	V	VI	VII	VIII
Major7	**Minor7**	**Minor7**	**Major7**	**7**	**Minor7**	**Minor7♭5**	**Major7**
Cmaj7	Dm7	Em7	Fmaj7	G7	Am7	Bm7♭5	Cmaj7
Gmaj7	Am7	Bm7	Cmaj7	D7	Em7	F#m7♭5	Gmaj7
Dmaj7	Em7	F#m7	Gmaj7	A7	Bm7	C#m7♭5	Dmaj7
Amaj7	Bm7	C#m7	Dmaj7	E7	F#m7	G#m7♭5	Amaj7
Emaj7	F#m7	G#m7	Amaj7	B7	C#m7	D#m7♭5	Emaj7
Bmaj7	C#m7	D#m7	Emaj7	F#7	G#m7	A#m7♭5	Bmaj7
F#maj7	G#m7	A#m7	Bmaj7	C#7	D#m7	E#(F)m7♭5	F#maj7
Fmaj7	Gm7	Am7	B♭maj7	C7	Dm7	Em7♭5	Fmaj7
B♭maj7	Cm7	Dm7	E♭maj7	F7	Gm7	Am7♭5	B♭maj7
E♭maj7	Fm7	Gm7	A♭maj7	B♭7	Cm7	Dm7♭5	E♭maj7
A♭maj7	B♭m7	Cm7	D♭maj7	E♭7	Fm7	Gm7♭5	A♭maj7
D♭maj7	E♭m7	Fm7	G♭maj7	A♭7	B♭m7	Cm7♭5	D♭maj7
G♭maj7	A♭m7	B♭m7	C♭(B) maj7	D♭7	E♭m7	Fm7♭5	G♭maj7

LESSON FORTY TWO

MODES

When improvising or writing melodies with a major scale, it is possible to start or finish on **any** note of the scale, i.e. you don't have to start on the first degree of the scale. By starting and ending on degrees other than **1**, different versions of the scale called **modes** are created. **Seven** different modes can be derived from the major scale by starting on each of the seven degrees of the scale. These modes were first used in ancient Greece and have been widely used throughout history in all types of music. They are particularly useful for improvising or composing melodies over chord progressions. The names of the seven modes and their relationship to the major scale are shown below.

1. Ionian – The Ionian mode is another name for the major scale itself. By starting and ending on the first note of the major scale (in this case **C**) you can play the Ionian mode.

C Ionian = C D E F G A B C

2. Dorian – The Dorian mode starts and ends on the second note of the major scale (in this case **D**).

D Dorian = D E F G A B C D

3. Phrygian – The Phrygian mode starts and ends on the third note of the major scale (in this case **E**).

E Phrygian = E F G A B C D E

4. Lydian – The Lydian mode starts and ends on the fourth note of the major scale (in this case **F**).

F Lydian = F G A B C D E F

5. Mixolydian – The Mixolydian mode starts and ends on the fifth note of the major scale (in this case **G**).

G Mixolydian = G A B C D E F G

6. Aeolian – The Aeolian mode starts and ends on the sixth note of the major scale (in this case **A**).

A Aeolian = A B C D E F G A

7. Locrian – The Locrian mode starts and ends on the seventh note of the major scale (in this case **B**).

B Locrian = B C D E F G A B

MODES IN ALL KEYS

The seven different modes can be derived **any** major scale, not just C major. The order of modes remains the same, but the starting note for each one will be different from one key to the next. The following example demonstrates the seven modes derived from the **B♭** major scale. Listen to how well each one works over its particular scale tone 7th chord. This is because the note on each beat of the bar is a note of the arpeggio of its corresponding chord. The other notes of each mode can be thought of as passing notes.

65.   Modes Derived From B♭ Major

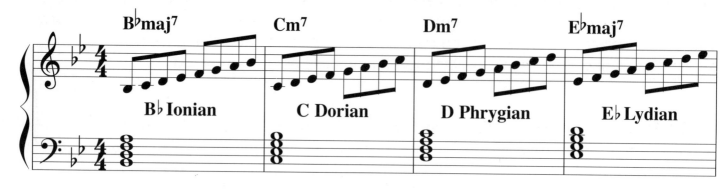

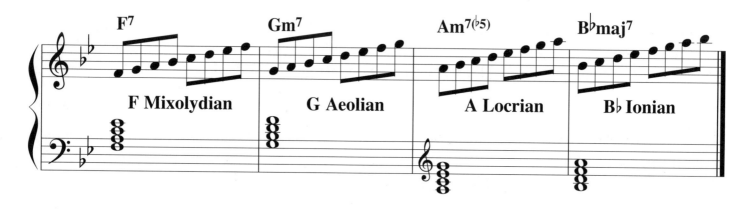

MODE FORMULAS

Any note of the chromatic scale can be used as a starting note for any mode. This requires a knowledge of the formula for each mode. These are listed below as scale degrees.

Ionian = 1 2 3 4 5 6 7

Dorian = 1 2 ♭3 4 5 6 ♭7

Phrygian = 1 ♭2 ♭3 4 5 ♭6 ♭7

Lydian = 1 2 3 ♯4 5 6 7

Mixolydian = 1 2 3 4 5 6 ♭7

Aeolian = 1 2 ♭3 4 5 ♭6 ♭7

Locrian = 1 ♭2 ♭3 4 ♭5 ♭6 ♭7

MODAL TONALITIES

Even though all these modes are derived from the major scale, it is possible to create sounds from some of the modes which are very different to the major scale. The following example demonstrates a melody created from the **C dorian** mode. This mode is particularly useful for minor key progressions where the $\overline{IV}$ chord is major, or dominant 7th, as demonstrated in the following example. Notice that the tonality is nothing like a major key even though all the notes are contained in the B♭ major scale. This example would be described as having a **modal** (in this case, Dorian) **tonality**.

 66.0 Dorian Tonality

 66.1 Phrygian Tonality

This one has a **Phrygian Tonality**. Try other modal tonalities by playing the accompanying scale tone chord (e.g. chord $\overline{IV}$Maj7 for lydian, $\overline{V}$7 for mixolydian, etc.) repeatedly with the left hand while improvising with the right hand using the notes of the mode.

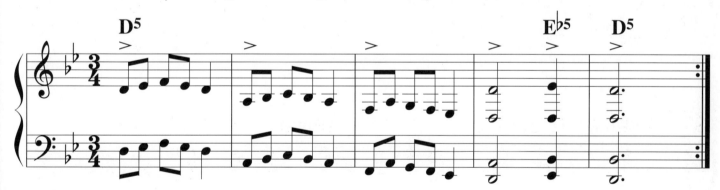

 66.2 Modes Over $\overline{I}$ $\overline{VI}$ $\overline{II}$ $\overline{V}$ in B♭

Once you are comfortable with the modes, try improvising with them over a chord progression as demonstrated in this example. The progression here is $\overline{I}$ $\overline{VI}$ $\overline{II}$ $\overline{V}$.

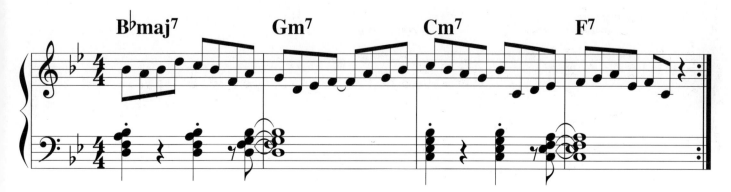

188

MODULATION

Although a particular key signature appears at the start, it is common to move to other keys during a piece of music. This is called **modulation**. The most common modulations are between relative major and minor, and between keys which are close together in the key cycle, but it is possible to move freely from any key to any other key as long as it sounds good. The following ballad in the key of **B♭ major** modulates to several other keys before returning to **B♭** major at the end. Notice the use of ₵ time here.

67. The Story Never Ends

Chris Martin

LESSON FORTY THREE

EXTENDED CHORDS

When you play Jazz, Funk, Fusion, or Modern R&B, you will often find chords which extend past the 7th, notably the various types of **9th**, **11th** and **13th** chords. These higher numbers come about by repeating the scale from which they are derived over two octaves. Thus, in the higher octave the 2nd becomes the 9th, the 4th becomes the 11th and the 6th becomes the 13th as shown below in the key of C.

C	D	E	F	G	A	B	C	D	E	F	G	A	B	C
1	2	3	4	5	6	7	8	9	10	11	12	13	14	15

As you learnt earlier in the book, most chords are made up of various 3rd intervals stacked one on top of the other. This means that by going through a scale in thirds (i.e. skipping every second note) it is easy to create chords up to a 13th. A **major triad** contains the degrees **1**, **3** and **5** of the major scale. A **major 7th** chord is created by adding the **7th** degree on top of the major triad. This 7th degree is a 3rd above the 5th of the chord. By adding another 3rd on top of the major 7th chord, a **major 9th** chord is created. By adding another 3rd on top of the major 9th chord, a **major 11th chord** is created. If you add another 3rd on top of the major 11th chord, a **major 13th** chord is created. The 13th is as high as the chord can go, because if you add a 3rd on top of the major 13th chord, you end up with the tonic of the chord again.

Depending on the nature of the 3rd and 7th degrees of the chord, 9ths 11ths and 13ths may be either major, minor or dominant in quality. E.g. if you add a **9th degree** on top of a **dominant 7th** chord, you end up with a **dominant 9th** chord (usually just called a 9th chord). If you add a 9th degree on top of a **minor 7th** chord, you end up with **a minor 9th** chord, etc. Written below are the formulas for some typical 9th, 11th and 13th chords.

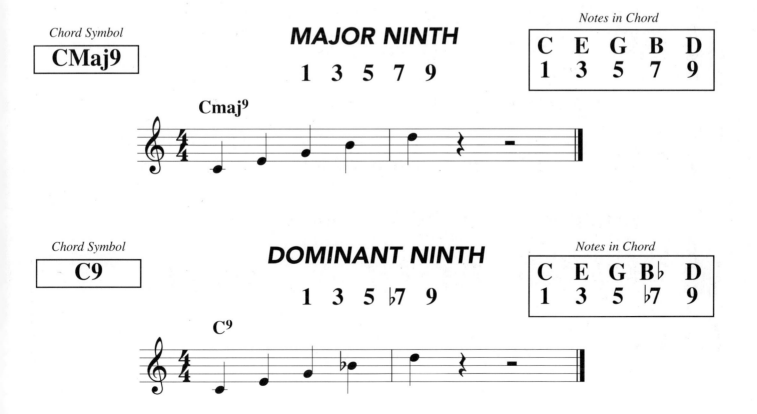

Chord Symbol

CMaj9

MAJOR NINTH

1 3 5 7 9

Notes in Chord

C	E	G	B	D
1	3	5	7	9

Cmaj⁹

Chord Symbol

C9

DOMINANT NINTH

1 3 5 ♭7 9

Notes in Chord

C	E	G	B♭	D
1	3	5	♭7	9

C⁹

 **68.0**

Here is an example demonstrating these three ninth chords. Play the root of each chord (**C**) with the left hand and the other notes with the right hand.

USING 7TH CHORDS TO CREATE 9THS

In lesson 41 you learnt to create scale tone 7th chords by choosing a bass note and using the triad two degrees ahead on top of the bass note. The same principle can be applied to creating 9th chords. E.g. if you place an **Em7 chord** over a **C bass note**, the result is a **CMaj9** chord as shown below. The example which follows uses this method to create a II̅ V̅ I̅ progression in the **key of C** where all three chords add up to **9ths**.

Em7 Chord ⟶ D B G E / C = D B G E C ⟵ C Maj9 Chord

C Bass Note ⟶

 **68.1** II̅ V̅ I̅ in C using 9ths

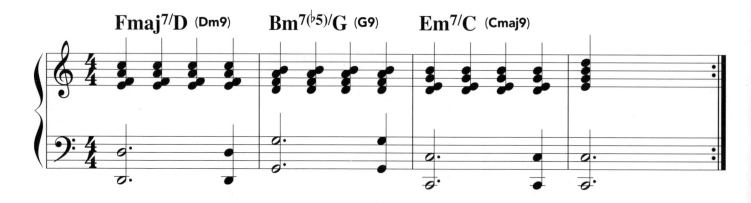

ELEVENTH CHORDS

By adding another 3rd interval on top of a 9th chord, it is possible to create an 11th chord. Depending on the 3rd and 7th of the chord, you can create major, minor and dominant 11th chords. The chord shown below is a C minor 11th (**Cm11**). By raising the 3rd of the chord from E♭ to E♮ it could be changed to a dominant 11th chord (**C11**). By raising the 3rd and the 7th it could be changed to a major 11th (**CMaj11**).

Chord Symbol		**MINOR ELEVENTH**			*Notes in Chord*					
Cm11		1 ♭3 5 ♭7 9 11			C	E♭	G	B♭	D	F
					1	♭3	5	♭7	9	11

 **69.0**

The more notes there are in a chord, the more difficult it becomes to play. When using extended chords, it is common to play only the guide tones as shown here. The right hand plays the **11th**, ♭**7th** and ♭**3rd** of the **Cm11** chord.

 **69.1**

When playing Major or Dominant **11th** chords, the 3rd and 11th (= 4th) degrees have the potential to clash and sound bad as shown in the first and second bars of the following example. For this reason it is common to leave out the 3rd degree when playing 11th chords, as shown in the final three bars of the example. The **C11** chord without the 3rd is created here by using a **Gm7** chord over a **C** bass note.

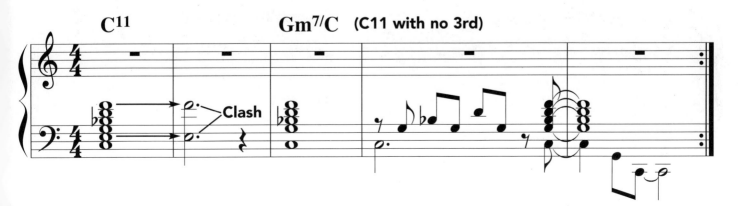

SUSPENDED 7TH CHORDS

Most times a dominant 11th chord is indicated in the music, you can substitute a **suspended 7th chord**. The formula for a suspended 7th chord is **1 4 5 ♭7**. This is simply a dominant 7th with the 3rd degree raised one semitone (suspended above the 3rd). The symbol for a suspended 7th chord is **7sus** or **7sus⁴**. Notice that the **Gm7/C** chord contains the same notes. Every chord you know can be used in a variety of ways. Experiment!

SHARP 11 CHORDS

Another way to get around the clash between the 3rd and 11th degrees is to **sharpen the 11th**. This is particularly common in Jazz. It works for any kind of extended chord, e.g. **7♯11**, **9♯11** and **13♯11**. The use of sharpened 11ths in a Major chord type strongly suggest a **Lydian tonality**, as demonstrated in the following example.

THIRTEENTH CHORDS

By adding another 3rd interval on top of an 11th chord, various types of 13th chords can be created. Once again depending on the 3rd and 7th of the chord, you can create major, minor and dominant 13th chords. The chord shown below is a C dominant 13th (**C13**). By flattening the 3rd of the chord it could be changed to a minor 13th chord (**Cm13**). By raising the 7th it could be changed to a major 13th (**CMaj13**).

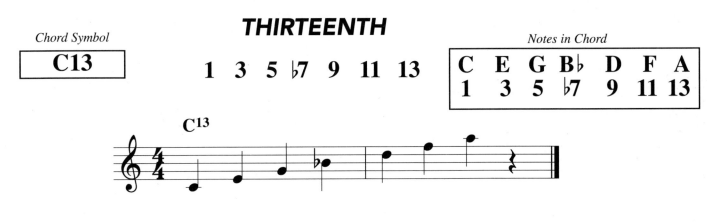

Chord Symbol											Notes in Chord						
C13		**THIRTEENTH**		1	3	5	♭7	9	11	13		C	E	G	B♭	D	F	A
												1	3	5	♭7	9	11	13

When playing dominant or major 13th chords, the 11th is either sharpened, or left out as in this example where the right hand plays only the **3**, **♭7** and **13**.

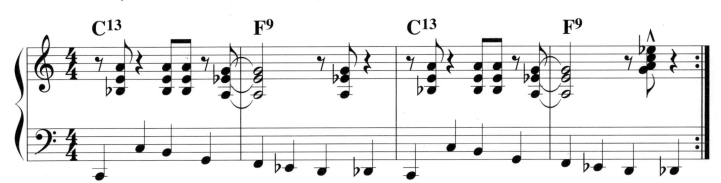

SIXTH CHORDS

Another common chord type is the sixth chord. These are four note chords consisting of a either a major or minor triad with an added 6th degree instead of a 7th. The chord symbols for 6th chords are self explanatory, e.g **C6** for a C major sixth or **Cm6** for a C minor sixth. The difference between a sixth chord and a thirteenth chord is that a thirteenth contains a **7th** degree as well as a 6th. Here is an example using major 7th chords.

13th implied by 7th in bass line

Here are two pieces which demonstrate common uses of extended chords. The first is a Jazz Blues in the key of **G**. Listen to the CD several times to get the feel of the rhythm and then work slowly through the piece until you can play it without hesitating. Then work on in with a metronome, gradually increasing the tempo until you can play it along with the CD. This type of playing works well for accompanying a vocalist or soloist. In Jazz, accompanying is called **comping**. This is a combination of accompanying and complementing.

71. Sonny's Bop

Chris Martin

72. An Oscar For Oscar

Chris Martin

This one is a Jazz solo in the key of F. Notice the use of secondary dominants in this piece to create modulations. Notice also the new chord symbols containing flattened **9th** and **13th** degrees. These are examples of **altered chords** which is the subject of lesson 45.

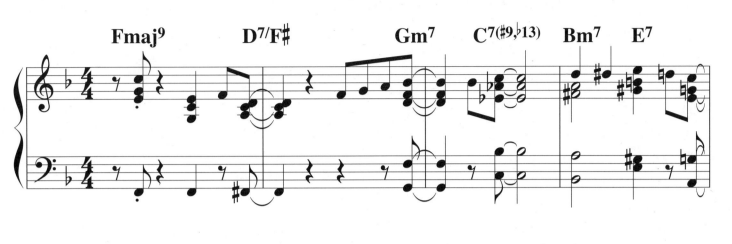

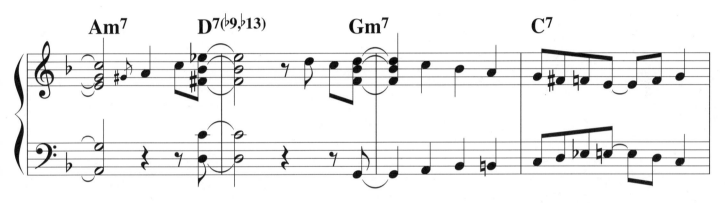

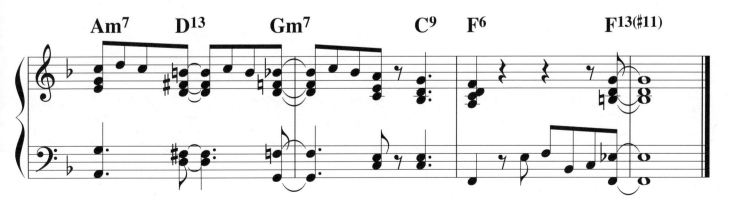

In discussing chord types, we have concentrated mainly on Jazz and Rock. However, all these chords can be found in the variety of styles that come under the general heading of Classical music. Here is a Prelude by **Bach** which uses many of the chords you have learnt. On the recording it is played with an electric piano voice and accompanied with synthesizer sounds.

73. **Prelude in C Major**

J.S. Bach

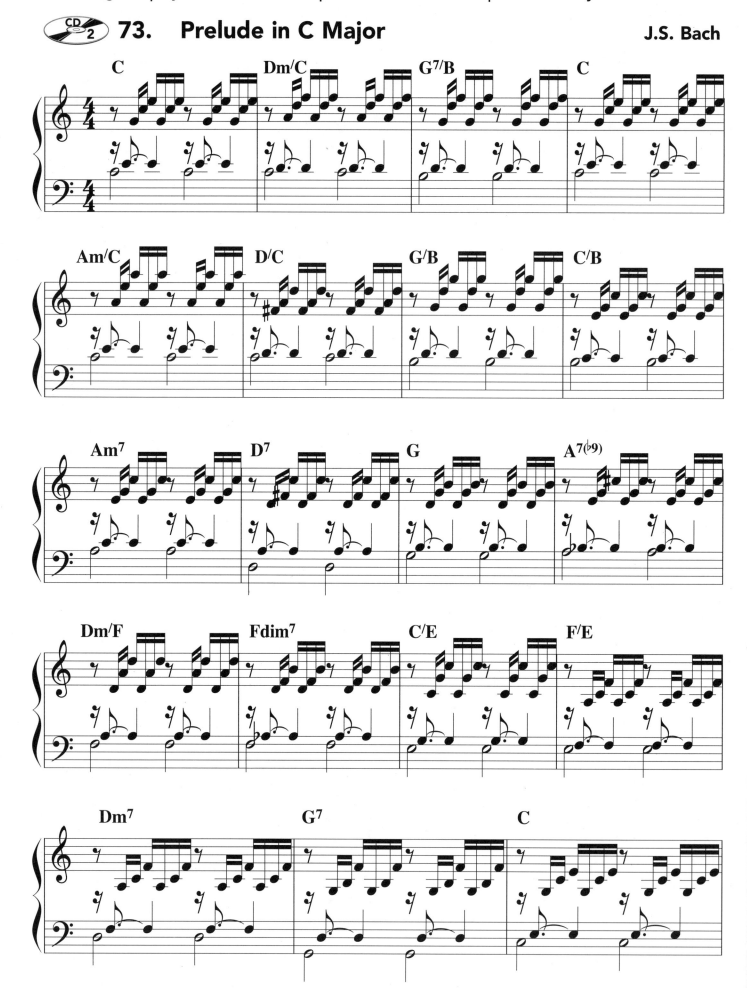

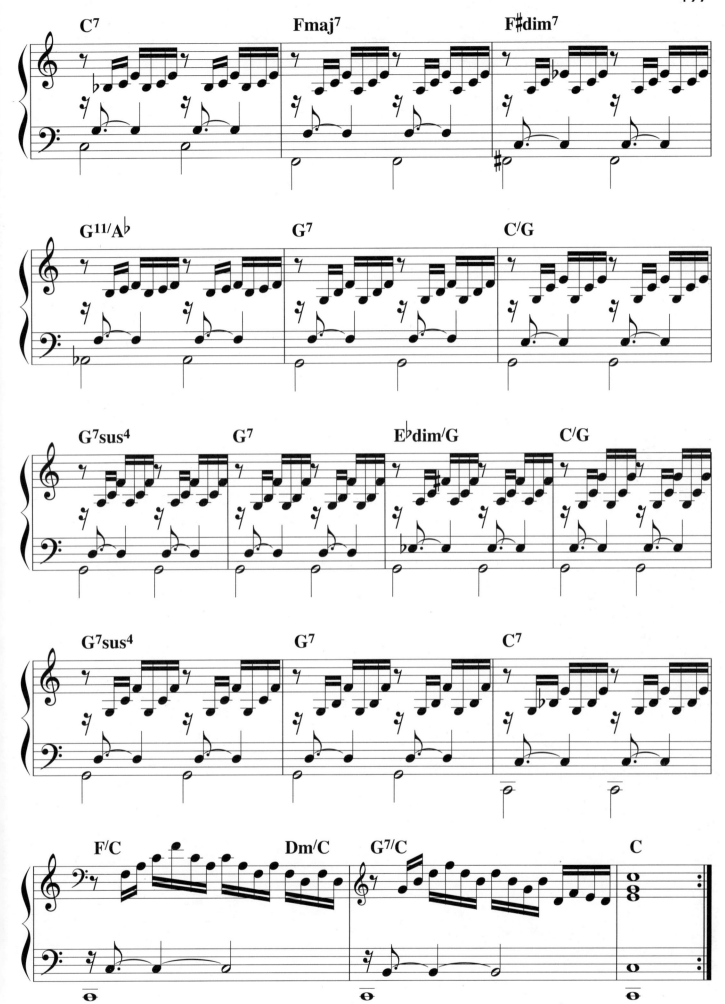

LESSON FORTY FOUR

HOW TO LEARN A NEW KEY

To become a good musician, it is essential to learn how to play fluently in every key. Once you know which notes are in the scale of a key you are not familiar with, the next step is to transfer the knowledge to your instrument until you can instantly find any note of the scale on the keyboard and build any chord type on any degree of the scale.

Let's take the key of **D major** as an example. The notes of the scale are written below. Notice that there are two sharps in this key – **F♯** and **C♯**.

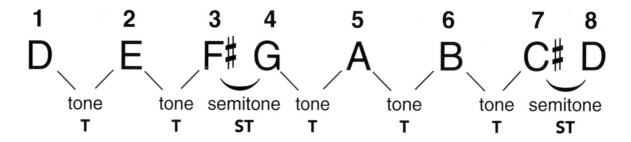

Here is the **D major scale** played over three octaves with both hands. Learn it from memory and then play it with your eyes closed, naming each note as you play and visualising the notation in your mind. Once you can do this, name the scale degrees as you play instead of the note names. If you have trouble with it, practice one hand at a time and then combine the hands.

74.0

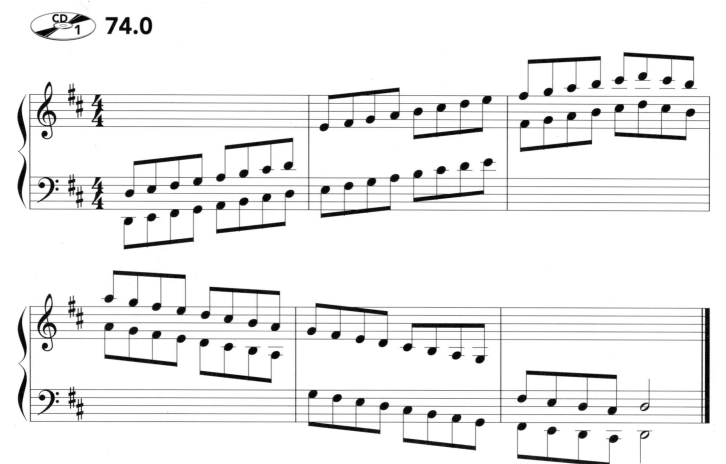

Once you are confident you can instantly find any note of the scale you are working on, try playing some **sequences** with the notes of the scale. Once again, work towards memorizing each new pattern and then play it with your eyes closed while naming first the notes and then the scale degrees. Here is an example.

 **74.1**

As well as individual notes, it is essential to know the scale tone chords of a key and to be able to move freely between them with either hand or both hands together. This example demonstrates all inversions of the scale tone triads of D major played with the left hand while the right hand plays the root of each chord.

 **75. D Major Scale Tone Triads**

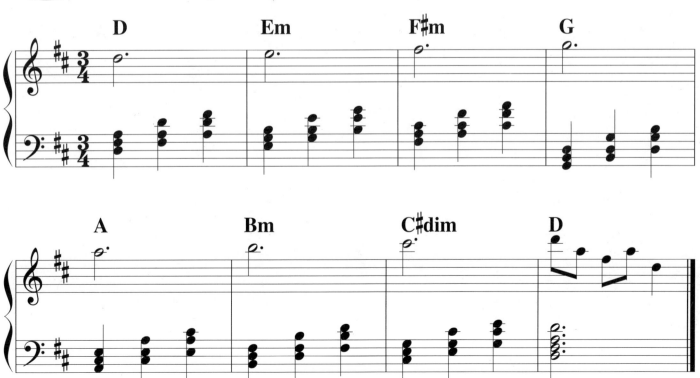

Once you are comfortable with the scale tone triads of a key, the next step is to use them to play chord progressions. Here are some examples. Notice the use of a **dominant 7th** for chord $\bar{V}$. It is important to practice chord $\bar{V}$ as both a triad and a 7th.

76.0 ($\bar{I}$ $\overline{IV}$ $\bar{V}$ $\bar{I}$)

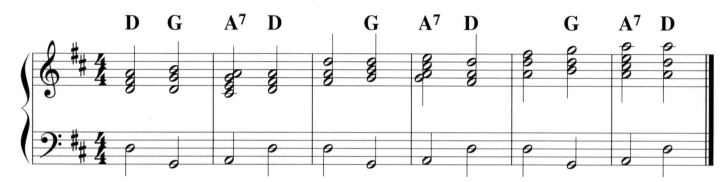

76.1 ($\bar{I}$ $\overline{VI}$ $\bar{II}$ $\bar{V}$)

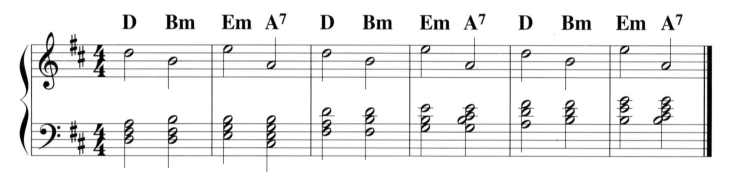

76.2 ($\bar{I}$ $\overline{IV}$ $\overline{VII}$ $\overline{III}$ $\overline{VI}$ $\bar{II}$ $\bar{V}$)

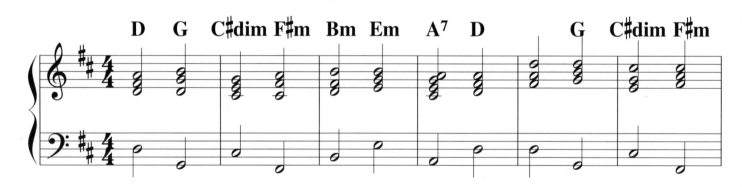

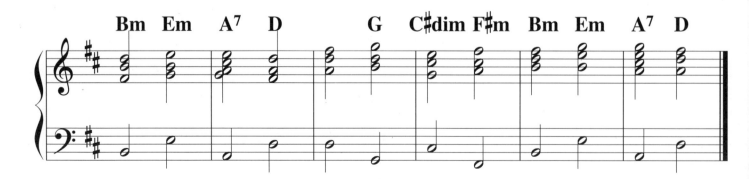

77. Scale Tone Triad Arpeggios in D

It is also important to know your scale tone chords as arpeggios. Here they are in the key of D over two octaves. This example uses a triplet rhythm, but practice them with eighth notes and sixteenth notes as well.

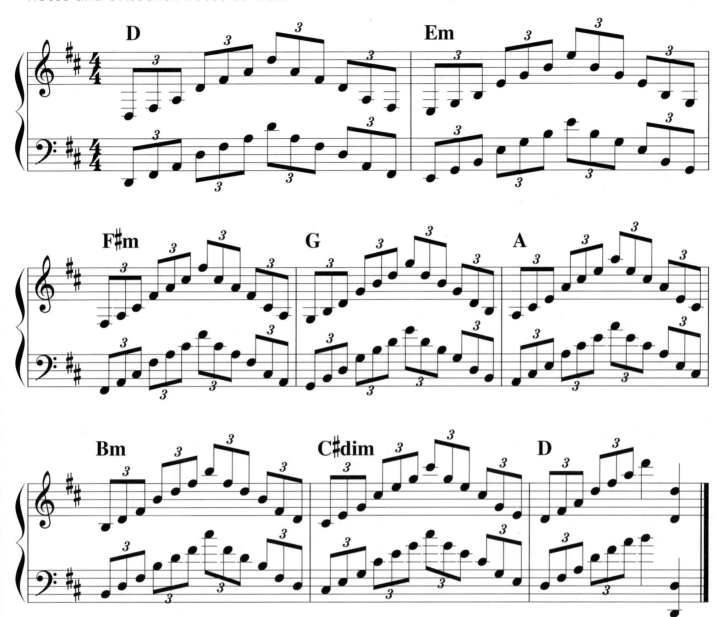

78. Improvising With Scale Tone Arpeggios

Once you know the arpeggios, the next step is using them to improvise over chord progressions. You need to be able to move freely from any note of an arpeggio to another rather than always running up and down through the chord.

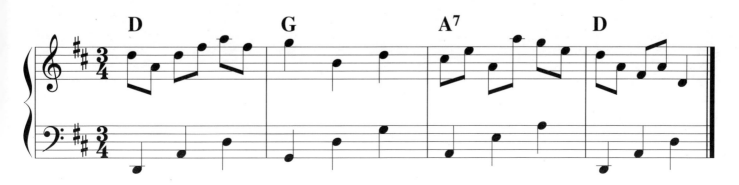

Another important step in learning a new key is to write your own parts in the key. A good way to do this is to concentrate on a particular interval. The following example features the use of **major and minor 2nd** intervals in the right hand part.

 **79.0**

 **79.1**

This example uses **major and minor 3rds**.

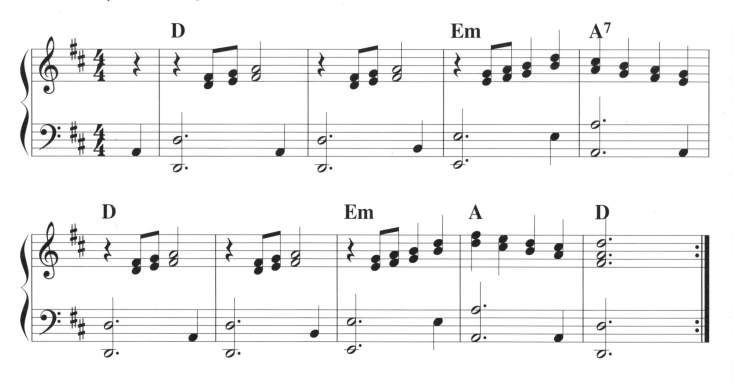

 **79.2**

This one features **major and minor 6ths**. Experiment with other intervals too.

80. Song for Everyone

Chris Martin

The other essential for learning a key is to play many songs and pieces in that key.

Remember that every key signature applies to both a major key and its relative minor. Here are the three types of minor scales for the key of **B minor** which is the relative of D Major.

81. 3 Scales in B Minor

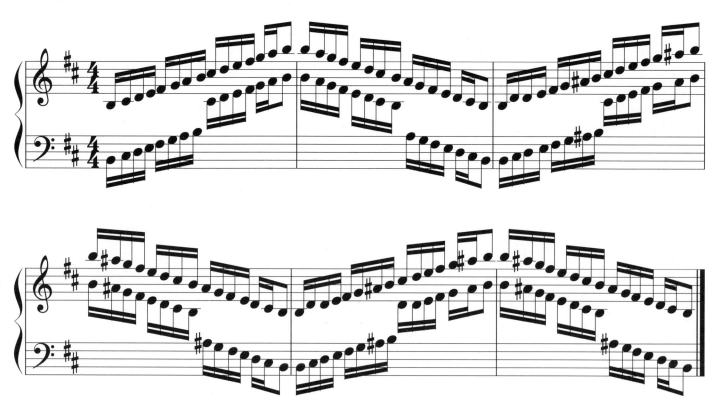

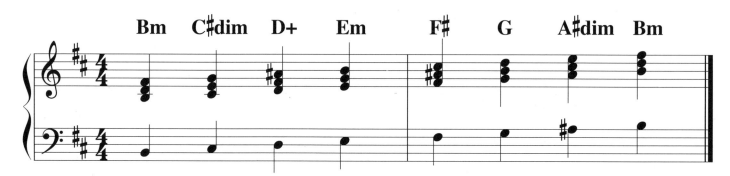

82. B Harmonic Minor Scale Tone Triads

Here are the scale tone triads derived from the **B harmonic minor** scale. Learn them in root position and then in all inversions as well as the arpeggios.

83.

As with the major key, it is important to use the chords of the relative minor in various ways over chord progressions. This example is a simple part using chords $\bar{I}$, $\overline{IV}$ and $\overline{V7}$ in B minor.

SCALE TONE SEVENTHS IN D

To play any kind of modern music you need to know all the upper extensions for chords in every key. The starting point for this is the scale tone 7ths. Here they are in **D major**. As with previous chords, learn them in root position, then in inversions and as arpeggios, and use them to play through many chord progressions in the key you are working on, e.g. II V I, I VI II V and I IV VII III VI II V.

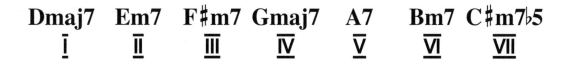

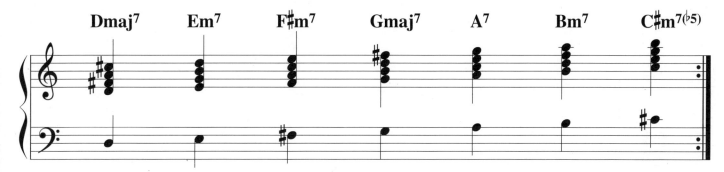

EXTENDED CHORDS IN D

The next step is to create extended chords by adding 3rd intervals above the scale tone sevenths. The following example is a comping part in the key of **D** using extended chords.

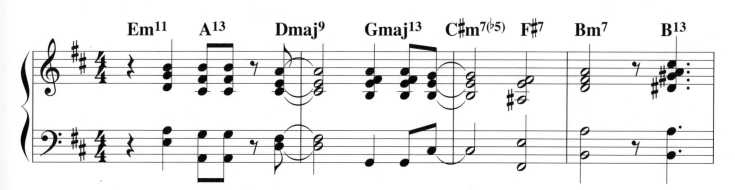

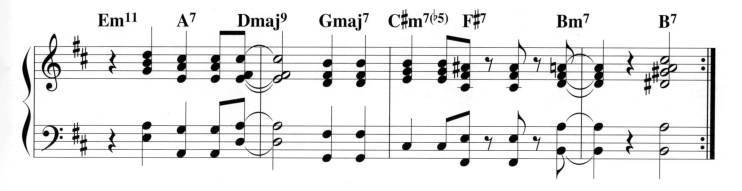

A great way to learn any key better is to transpose pieces you already know to that key. Shown below is the Jazz solo from page 195 transposed to the key of **D**. You originally learnt this piece in the key of F. Transposing something like this takes quite a bit of knowledge, so remember that learning all the keys is a **long term project**. Spend a short time on it each day and gradually your confidence in each key will grow more secure.

86.   **An Oscar For Oscar (Key of D)**   Chris Martin

Whenever you jam with other musicians, it's likely that the **Blues** will be involved at some point. Being able to play the Blues in all keys is a basic requirement for a Jazz musician. To learn to play Blues in a new key, start by learning chords $\bar{I}$, $\overline{IV}$ and $\overline{V}$ of the key as dominant 7ths (**D7**, **G7** and **A7** in the **key of D**) and using them to play through the 12 bar Blues form. Then learn the Blues scale in that key and improvise with it over a simple left hand pattern. Go through the earlier lessons on Blues playing and transpose all the examples to the key of D, and eventually to all the other keys as well. The following Blues uses a new left hand pattern which is a variation on one you already know.

87.   Hold That Train

LESSON FORTY FIVE

ALTERED CHORDS

Another thing you will find in all modern music styles is the use of **altered chords**. The flattening or raising of 3rds and 7ths is common in basic chord construction, but the other degrees of a chord may also be raised or lowered. The most common altered chords involve alterations to the **5th** and/or the **9th**. Usually the alteration appears in the name of the chord. Some examples are given below.

SEVEN SHARP NINE CHORD FORMULA

Chord Symbol

C7#9

$$1 \quad 3 \quad 5 \quad \flat7 \quad \#9$$

Notes in Chord

C	E	G	B♭	D#
1	3	5	♭7	#9

 **88.**

This example demonstrates the **7#9** chord, which is one of the most common altered chords. Only the essential notes are played by the right hand.

SEVEN FLAT FIVE
CHORD FORMULA

Chord Symbol

C7♭5

1   3   ♭5   ♭7

Notes in Chord

C	E	G♭	B♭
1	3	♭5	♭7

89.0

The **5th** can also be flattened or sharpened in extended chords. This example uses three altered chords - **D7♭5** , **E7♭9** and **E7♯9**.

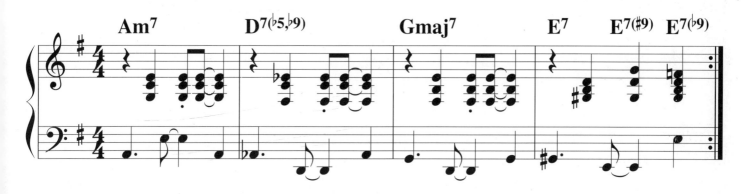

THIRTEENTH
SHARP 11 FORMULA

Chord Symbol

C13♯11

1   3   5   ♭7   9   ♯11   13

Notes in Chord

C	E	G	B♭	D	F♯	A
1	3	5	♭7	9	♯11	13

 **89.1**

Here's one featuring the **13♯11** chord. For a more in-depth study of altered chords, and extended chords in general, see *Complete Learn to Play Jazz Keyboard Manual*.

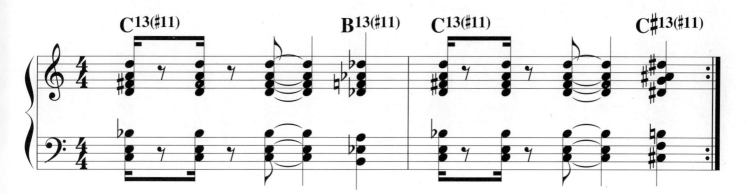

TENSION AND RELEASE

Once you have a new piece of knowledge, e.g. how to create altered chords, it is easy to get carried away and over-use your new knowledge. However, it is just as important to know when **not** to use something. Music is always a balance of **tension and release**. Altered chords are great for creating tension, so it makes sense to move from an altered chord to an unaltered chord to release that tension. Another way of using tension and release is to alternate between busy rhythmic sections and sparser sections containing more sustained notes, or rests. These things are demonstrated in the following example.

90. Back to the Street

Chris Martin

LESSON FORTY SIX

SCALE TONE 7THS IN MINOR KEYS

Shown below is an A natural minor scale harmonized as 7th chords. Remember that the chords will be exactly the same as those contained in the key of C major (the relative major key). The only difference is the starting and finishing point. Because the minor scale starts on A, **Am7** will now be chord $\overline{\text{I}}$ instead of $\overline{\text{VI}}$.

	G	A	B	C	D	E	F
	E	F	G	A	B	C	D
	C	D	E	F	G	A	B
	A	B	C	D	E	F	G
	$\overline{\text{I}}$	$\overline{\text{II}}$	$\overline{\text{III}}$	$\overline{\text{IV}}$	$\overline{\text{V}}$	$\overline{\text{VI}}$	$\overline{\text{VII}}$
Natural Minor	Am7	Bm7♭5	Cmaj7	Dm7	Em7	Fmaj7	G7

If you harmonize the harmonic or melodic minor scale, the chords will **not** be identical to those of the relative major. Shown below is the A harmonic minor harmonized as 7th chords. The raised 7th degree results in different chord types for chords $\overline{\text{I}}$ (a minor chord with a major 7th: **m/maj7**), $\overline{\text{III}}$, (a major 7th chord with a raised 5th: **maj7♯5**), $\overline{\text{V}}$ (a dominant 7th chord) and $\overline{\text{VII}}$ (a diminished 7th chord).

	G♯	A	B	C	D	E	F
	E	F	G♯	A	B	C	D
	C	D	E	F	G♯	A	B
	A	B	C	D	E	F	G♯
	$\overline{\text{I}}$	$\overline{\text{II}}$	$\overline{\text{III}}$	$\overline{\text{IV}}$	$\overline{\text{V}}$	$\overline{\text{VI}}$	$\overline{\text{VII}}$
Harmonic Minor	Am/maj7	Bm7♭5	Cmaj7♯5	Dm7	E7	Fmaj7	G♯°7

By harmonizing the ascending melodic minor scale, even more of the chords are altered. As you can see from the table below, none of the chords here are the same as those derived from the natural minor. The fact that there are three different minor scales gives you many chord options for harmonizing a melody in a minor key. This is discussed on the following page.

	G♯	A	B	C	D	E	F♯
	E	F♯	G♯	A	B	C	D
	C	D	E	F♯	G♯	A	B
	A	B	C	D	E	F♯	G♯
	$\overline{\text{I}}$	$\overline{\text{II}}$	$\overline{\text{III}}$	$\overline{\text{IV}}$	$\overline{\text{V}}$	$\overline{\text{VI}}$	$\overline{\text{VII}}$
Melodic Minor	Am/maj7	Bm7	Cmaj7♯5	D7	E7	F♯m7♭5	G♯m7♭5

HIGHER EXTENSIONS IN MINOR KEYS

Like major scale tone chords, it is possible to add 9ths, 11ths and 13ths to chords built on the notes of minor scales. Shown below are scale tone 9th chords built on an A harmonic minor scale. Notice that some of the chords are no longer straight minor, dominant or major 9ths, but have more complex names because of the alterations caused by the raised 7th degree of the harmonic minor scale (in this case, a **G#** note). These chords may seem confusing at first and may take a while to learn, but in the long run it is well worth it, as knowledge of these chords will help you improvise better and more easily in minor keys.

	B	C	D	E	F	G#	A
	G#	A	B	C	D	E	F
	E	F	G#	A	B	C	D
	C	D	E	F	G#	A	B
	A	B	C	D	E	F	G#
	$\underline{\text{I}}$	$\underline{\text{II}}$	$\underline{\text{III}}$	$\underline{\text{IV}}$	$\underline{\text{V}}$	$\underline{\text{VI}}$	$\underline{\text{VII}}$
Harmonic Minor	Am9/maj7	Bm7♭5♭9	Cmaj9♯5	Dm9	E7♭9	Fmaj7♯9	G#m6/9♭5

When harmonizing melodies in minor keys, some of the higher extensions are more commonly used than others. The most common is the use of the ♭**9** in chord $\underline{\text{V}}$. The following example demonstrates the use of this note in a minor key $\underline{\text{II}}$ $\underline{\text{V}}$ $\underline{\text{I}}$ progression.

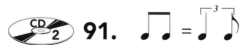

91.

SUBSTITUTIONS IN MINOR KEYS

All the types of substitution which apply to major keys (relative substitutions, scale tone triads or 7ths two degrees ahead in the key, dominant minor, and tritone substitutions) can be applied to minor keys as well. The main difference you will find is that when you start to go into the upper extensions of chords built on the harmonic and melodic minors, you will get alterations to the chords. Shown below are the chords resulting from substituting scale tone 7th chords two ahead for the standard scale tone 7ths of **A melodic minor**.

92.

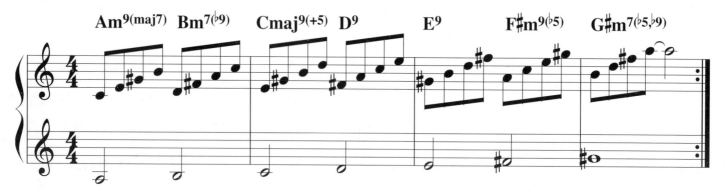

Here is a final Latin Jazz style piece in **A minor** featuring extended chords. Congratulations on finishing the book. You now have the tools to play any style of music. It is important to remember that chords, scales and arpeggios are just the building blocks. From here on you will make the most progress by playing with other musicians as often as possible. Happy playing!

93. The Brazilian

Chris Martin

LISTENING

Apart from books, your most important source of information as a musician is **recordings**. Listen to albums which feature piano or keyboard players. All music is an extension of what has come before it, so you need to be aware of the development of keyboard playing throughout the history of music. Studying **Classical** music will give you a solid grounding which can be used in any style of music. For more recent styles such as Jazz, Blues and Rock, it is essential to listen to a wide variety of players, some of whom are listed below. There is a lot of crossover between styles which come under the headings of Rock, Jazz, Blues, R&B and Funk. There are many great players in these styles, but the following list is a good start.

Blues: Otis Spann, Memphis Slim, Champion Jack Dupree, Dr John, James Booker, and Professor Longhair.

Soul/Gospel: Mildred Falls (with Mahalia Jackson - "Live at Newport 1958"), Ray Charles, Aretha Franklin, and Richard Tee.

Funk: Herbie Hancock, Art Neville (the Meters and the Neville Brothers), Bernie Worrell of Parliament/Funkadelic, Stevie Wonder, and George Duke.

Rock/Pop: Little Richard, Billy Powell of Lynyrd Skynyrd, Jon Lord (Deep Purple), Keith Emerson (Emerson, Lake and Palmer), Donald Fagen (Steely Dan), Leon Russell, Jackson Browne, Elton John, Billy Joel, Fiona Apple, Bruce Hornsby, Tori Amos, Ben Folds, and Vanessa Carlton.

Jazz: Jelly Roll Morton, Lil Hardin (with Louis Armstrong) Fats Waller, Teddy Wilson, Count Basie, Duke Ellington, Mary Lou Williams, Art Tatum, Thelonious Monk, Bud Powell, Horace Silver, Wynton Kelly, Red Garland, Oscar Peterson, Bill Evans, McCoy Tyner, Herbie Hancock (Jazz as well as Funk), Jimmy Smith (Hammond Organ), Keith Jarrett, Joe Zawinul (with Weather Report), Mike Nock, John Medeski, Jacky Terrason, and Brad Mehldau.

For more books and recordings by Peter Gelling, visit **www.bentnotes.com**

TRANSCRIBING, PLAYING WITH OTHERS

When you are listening to albums, try to sing along with the solos and rhythm parts, and visualize the fingerings and techniques you would use to achieve the sounds you are hearing. **Write down** anything you really like, or anything you can't immediately transfer from your ear to the keyboard. This is called **transcribing**. All the great players have done **lots** of it. Transcribing helps you to understand and absorb the music and before long, it starts to come out in your own playing. It is also valuable to play along with albums, sometimes imitating what you are hearing and other times improvising. This is great ear training and is lots of fun.

It is essential to play with other musicians as much as possible. This helps you use everything you learn in real musical situations. Playing with others is also the **only** way to develop the interaction which is essential for any musician.

AMPLIFICATION

When playing with a band, it is often difficult to hear an acoustic piano without amplification. There are microphones such as PZM's which are good for picking up the sound of a piano. The microphone can then be put through a PA system in a similar way to a vocal microphone. When using an electronic keyboard, it is much more common to plug it into an amplifier. Bass or guitar amplifiers can be used for keyboards, but it is usually better to use an amp specially designed for keyboards. If you are uncertain about an amp, it is always better to consult a professional before deciding what to buy.

GLOSSARY OF MUSICAL TERMS

Accidental — a sign used to show a temporary change in pitch of a note (i.e. sharp ♯ , flat ♭ , double sharp ✗ , double flat ♭♭ , or natural ♮). The sharps or flats in a key signature are not regarded as accidentals.

Ad lib — to be played at the performer's own discretion.

Anacrusis — a note or notes occurring before the first bar of music (also called 'lead-in' notes).

Arpeggio — the playing of a chord in single note fashion.

Bar — a division of music occurring between two bar lines (also called a 'measure').

Bar line — a vertical line drawn across the staff which divides the music into equal sections called bars.

Chord — a combination of three or more different notes played together.

Chord progression — a series of chords played as a musical unit (e.g. as in a song).

Chromatic scale — a scale ascending and descending in semitones.
e.g. **C** chromatic scale:

ascending: C   C♯   D   D♯   E   F   F♯   G   G♯   A   A♯   B   C

descending: C   B   B♭   A   A♭   G   G♭   F   E   E♭   D   D♭   C

Common time —   and indication of ⁴⁄₄ time — four quarter note beats per bar (also indicated by 𝄴)

D.C al fine — a repeat from the sign (indicated thus 𝄋) to the word 'fine

Duration — the time value of each note.

Dynamics — the varying degrees of softness (indicated by the term 'piano') and loudness (indicated by the term 'forte') in music.

Eighth note — a note with the value of half a beat in ⁴⁄₄ time, indicated thus ♪ (also called a quaver).

Eighth rest — indicating half a beat of silence is written: 𝄾

Enharmonic — describes the difference in notation, but not in pitch, of two notes: e.g.

F♯ or G♭

First and second endings — signs used where two different endings occur. On the first time through ending one is played (indicated by the bracket ⌐1⎯⎯⎯⎤); then the progression is repeated and ending two is played (indicated ⌐2⎯⎯⎯⎤).

Harmony — the simultaneous sounding of two or more different notes.

Improvise — to perform spontaneously; i.e. not from memory or from a written copy.

Interval — the distance between any two notes of different pitches.

Key — describes the notes used in a composition in regards to the major or minor scale from which they are taken; e.g. a piece 'in the key of C major' describes the melody, chords, etc., as predominantly consisting of the notes, **C, D, E, F, G, A,** and **B** — i.e. from the **C** scale.

Key signature — a sign, placed at the beginning of each stave of music, directly after the clef, to indicate the key of a piece. The sign consists of a certain number of sharps or flats, which represent the sharps or flats found in the scale of the piece's key. e.g.

 indicates a scale with **F♯** and **C♯** , which is **D** major; **D E F♯ G A B C♯ D**. Therefore the key is **D** major.

Lead-In — same as anacrusis (also called a pick-up).
Leger lines — small horizontal lines upon which notes are written when their pitch is either above or below the range of the staff, e.g.

Legato — smoothly, well connected.
Major scale — a series of eight notes in alphabetical order based on the interval sequence tone - tone - semitone - tone - tone - tone - semitone, giving the familiar sound **do re mi fa so la ti do**.
Melody — a succession of notes of varying pitch and duration, and having a recognizable musical shape.
Metronome — a device which indicates the number of beats per minute, and which can be adjusted in accordance to the desired tempo.

e.g. **MM** (Maelzel Metronome) ♩ = 60 — indicates 60 quarter note beats per minute.
Natural — a sign (♮)used to cancel our the effect of a sharp or flat. The word is also used to describe the notes **A, B, C, D, E, F** and **G**; e.g. 'the natural notes'.
Octave — the distance between any given note with a set frequency, and another note with exactly double that frequency. Both notes will have the same letter name;

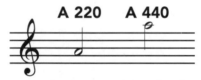

Pitch — the sound produced by a note, determined by the frequency of the string vibrations. The pitch relates to a note being referred to as 'high' or 'low'.
Repeat signs — in music, used to indicate a repeat of a section of music, by means of two dots placed before a double bar line:

In chord progressions, a repeat sign 𝄍 , indicates and exact repeat of the previous bar.
Semitone — the smallest interval used in conventional music.
Sharp — a sign (♯) used to raise the pitch of a note by one semitone.
Staccato — to play short and detached. Indicated by a dot placed above the note:
Staff — five parallel lines together with four spaces, upon which music is written.
Syncopation — displacing the normal flow of accents in music. Usually from on the beat to off the beat.
Tempo — the speed of a piece.
Tie — a curved line joining two or more notes of the same pitch, where the second note(s) is not played, but its time value is added to that of the first note.

(1)

(2)

Timbre — a quality which distinguishes a note produced on one instrument from the same note produced on any other instrument (also called 'tone colour'). A given note on the guitar will sound different (and therefore distinguishable) from the same pitched note on piano, violin, flute etc.
Transposition — the process of changing music from one key to another.